al fresco

RYLAND
PETERS
& SMALL
London New York

al fresco

Louise Pickford *photography by* Ian Wallace

First published in the United States in 2002
by Ryland Peters & Small, Inc.
519 Broadway, 5th Floor
New York, NY 10012
www.rylandpeters.com

10 9 8 7 6 5 4 3 2 1

ISBN 1 84172 249 9

Library of Congress Cataloging-in-Publication Data

Pickford, Louise.
  Al fresco / Louise Pickford ; photography by
Ian Wallace.
    p. cm.
  Includes index.
  ISBN 1-84172-249-9
  1. Picnicking. 2. Outdoor cookery. I. Title.

TX823 .P47 2002
641.8'78–dc21   2001048715

Notes

All spoon measurements are level unless
otherwise specified.

Ovens should be preheated to the specified
temperature. Recipes in this book were tested
in a regular oven. If using a convection oven,
decrease the oven temperature by 40°F, or
follow the manufacturer's instructions.

Uncooked or partially cooked eggs should not be
served to the very old, the very young, pregnant
women, or to those whose health is compromised.

Senior Designer Steve Painter
Commissioning Editor Elsa Petersen-Schepelern
Production Meryl Silbert
Art Director Gabriella Le Grazie
Publishing Director Alison Starling

Food Stylist Louise Pickford
Props Stylist Heidi Castles
Indexer Hilary Bird

Acknowledgments

The author and publisher would like to thank Keith
& Louise Matheny for allowing us to photograph
aboard their boat M.V. Hattitude in Sydney, and
Les Reedman and Helen Robbins for allowing us
to photograph at their homes. Thanks also to
Cleopatra Blue Mountains, a Relais & Chateaux
property of five guest rooms and restaurant in the
Blue Mountains outside Sydney, NSW, Australia.
Beautiful props were lent to us by Mosmania, of
Mosman, NSW; Bison Homewares, of Deakin in
the Australian Capital Territory (www.bisonhome.
com.au), Room Interior Products of Melbourne and
New York (www.room.com.au), and Lucienne Linen
of Mosman, NSW (www.luciennelinens.com.au).
Our thanks for their assistance.

contents

eating al fresco

Al fresco means "in the open air" and is synonymous with eating outdoors. Why food tastes better outside is one of life's mysteries. Is it just being in the fresh air on a warm summer's day that is so pleasurable—and eating is merely a way to pass the time—or is there more to it? I definitely think food comes alive in the open air—the colors are more vivid, the smell more evocative, and the flavors more satisfying.

Since moving to Australia, I have come to appreciate the true meaning of al fresco eating. Every night during the summer, I see couples snuggled romantically on a bench sipping a glass of wine and sharing a snack, or groups of friends picnicking on a stretch of grass beside the harbor, watching the sunset.

Weekends at the beach are guaranteed to provide the perfect spot for a picnic or barbecue and, in many parks here, outdoor grills are a permanent fixture—you don't even have to worry about bringing your own: you just turn up with the food and coals and start cooking. Some public grills are even gas-fired: what could be simpler?

I have some great memories of picnics and barbecues in England, where the sometimes inclement weather would have us sheltering under a huge umbrella.

Somehow, it never really seemed to matter: we always had fun and the food still tasted great. Everybody loves eating outside, where we feel happier and healthier. You don't need a glorious view or sandy beach to enjoy it: a table in the backyard, on the deck, or on a roof terrace still provide us with an opportunity to eat in the fresh air.

It is the food that is important, that takes center stage. As a food writer, I can think of little more exciting than writing recipes that are intended to be eaten al fresco. I hope I have managed to assemble a collection of recipes that will inspire everyone to pack up a lunch and head out to the hills.

When planning this book, I tried to think of the kind of food that would be best suited to eating outdoors. Then I realized that was crazy, because all food tastes better in the open. The result is this collection of my favorite dishes. I have included a range of recipes from the quick and simple for an impromptu picnic, to some that are more involved and which you might like to serve at a special party. There are also some elaborate dishes designed to be eaten within range of the stove for a dinner party in the backyard or on the terrace.

Think how you love eating outdoors; lunch in the backyard, a barbecue on the beach, a picnic in the country, dinner beside the pool, a packed lunch to take on a hike, food to serve at a backyard cocktail party, brunch on the terrace—the list is endless.

brunch in the sun

Brunch is usually a weekend luxury. It offers us the perfect excuse to linger over breakfast, savoring the fact that we don't have to rush off to work. If it's a sunny morning, that's just the icing on the cake.

Set a tray with your favorite brunch dishes and a large pot of steaming hot coffee or tea. Tuck the newspapers under your arm and head out onto the terrace or deck, or into the yard. Sit in the sun—if that's what you like to do—or snooze in the shade to save your complexion.

Brunch can be marvelous as a solitary indulgence for just yourself and your partner, but it's also a great excuse for casual entertaining. Invite your friends around to share an al fresco meal on a Saturday or Sunday. It sets the scene for a perfect day and, more often than not, brunch turns into a long lunch followed by a relaxing afternoon and, before we know it, early evening drinks—all outdoors. Sounds good enough to eat!

berries with honeyed yogurt

8 oz. fresh blueberries,
about 1¾ cups

a strip of lemon zest

a squeeze of lemon juice

a pinch of ground cinnamon

2¾ cups plain yogurt
(not low-fat)

⅓ cup honey

Serves 4–6

Since I moved to Sydney, with its wonderful sunny climate, I've discovered the joys of brunch or breakfast eaten outdoors. Breakfast is big in this city, with hundreds of cafés, bistros, and bars offering wonderfully light, healthy food to people en route to work. This recipe was inspired by a dish I discovered at one of my favorite places—a café in Balmoral, a pretty beachside suburb.

Reserve a few of the best berries for serving and put the remainder into a saucepan. Add the lemon zest, lemon juice, cinnamon, and 1 tablespoon water. Heat gently for about 3 minutes until the berries just start to soften slightly. Let cool.

Spoon the berries into glasses, then add the yogurt and honey. Top with the reserved berries and serve.

Creamy scrambled eggs topped with arugula pesto are especially good with the extra crunch provided by a nut bread or one made with extra seeds and oat flakes.

12 eggs

¼ cup heavy cream

4 tablespoons butter

6 slices bread, toasted (preferably walnut bread)

salt and freshly ground black pepper

Arugula pesto

2 oz. arugula

2 tablespoons chopped fresh basil

2 tablespoons blanched almonds, chopped

⅓ cup extra virgin olive oil

1 garlic clove, chopped

2 tablespoons freshly grated pecorino or Parmesan cheese

salt and freshly ground black pepper

Serves 6

creamy eggs
with arugula pesto

To make the pesto, chop the arugula coarsely, then transfer to a food processor. Add the basil, almonds, oil, garlic, salt, and pepper, and purée briefly to form a vivid green paste. Transfer to a bowl and stir in the cheese.

Put the eggs and cream into a bowl, beat with a fork, then add salt and pepper. Put the butter into a large nonstick saucepan, melt gently, then add the egg mixture and cook, stirring with a wooden fork or spoon over low heat until the eggs have just set.

Put a slice of toast onto each plate, add the scrambled eggs, and serve, topped with a spoonful of pesto.

honey-roasted peaches
with ricotta and coffee-bean sugar

Grinding whole coffee beans with a lump of sugar is typically Italian and adds a delicious crunch to the dish. This is a wonderful recipe, to be enjoyed on a warm summer morning.

6 large peaches or nectarines

2 tablespoons honey

1 tablespoon coffee beans

1 tablespoon sugar

1 ½ cups chilled ricotta cheese

Serves 6

Cut the peaches or nectarines in half and remove the pits. Line an ovenproof dish with parchment paper and add the peaches or nectarines, cut side up. Drizzle with the honey and roast in a preheated oven at 425°F for 15–20 minutes, until the fruit is tender and caramelized. Let cool slightly.

Put the coffee beans and sugar into a coffee grinder and grind very briefly, until the beans and sugar are coarsely ground.

Spoon the peaches or nectarines onto plates, top with a scoop of ricotta, sprinkle with the sugary coffee beans, then serve.

warm blueberry and almond **muffins**

Muffins are quick and easy to prepare and make a lovely breakfast snack, especially when served warm with coffee.

Sift the flour, baking powder, and apple pie spice into a bowl and stir in the ground almonds and sugar. Put the egg, buttermilk, and melted butter into a second bowl and beat well. Stir into the dry ingredients to make a smooth batter.

Fold in the blueberries, then spoon the mixture into 10 of the muffin cases in the muffin pan until three-quarters full. Scatter with the chopped almonds and bake in a preheated oven at 400°F for about 18–20 minutes, until risen and golden. Remove from the oven, let cool on a wire rack, and serve warm.

1¾ cups all-purpose flour

1½ teaspoons baking powder

1 teaspoon ground apple pie spice

½ cup ground almonds or ¾ cup slivered almonds, finely ground in a food processor

¾ cup sugar

1 egg

1¼ cups buttermilk

¼ cup butter, melted

8 oz. blueberries, about 2 cups

2 tablespoons almonds, chopped

12-cup muffin pan with paper muffin cases

Makes 10

pan bagnat

4 ciabatta rolls

2 garlic cloves, crushed

¼ cup extra virgin olive oil

1 tablespoon red wine vinegar

4 ripe tomatoes, thickly sliced

7 oz. canned tuna in olive oil,
drained and flaked

24 pitted black olives,
preferably niçoise

12 anchovy fillets in oil, drained

2 tablespoons capers

a few arugula leaves

a handful of basil leaves

salt and freshly ground
black pepper

Serves 4

Cut the ciabatta rolls in half. Put the garlic, oil and vinegar into a bowl, mix well, then brush all over the cut surfaces of the rolls.

Divide the remaining ingredients between the 4 rolls, add the lids, and wrap in plastic wrap. Let soak and infuse for at least 1 hour before serving.

warm potato tortilla
with smoked salmon

1 lb. small new potatoes

2 tablespoons butter

1 small onion, sliced

4 eggs

8 oz. smoked salmon

salt and freshly ground black pepper

smoked salmon, salmon caviar,
and crème fraîche, to serve

Serves 4

Cook the potatoes in a saucepan of lightly salted, boiling water for 10–12 minutes until cooked but not falling apart. Drain and refresh under cold water. Pat dry and cut into dice.

Put half the butter into a skillet, melt over a low heat, add the onion, and cook gently for 5 minutes. Add the potato slices and cook for 5 minutes more.

Put the eggs, salt, and pepper into a bowl, beat well, then stir in the potato and onion mixture. Put the remaining butter into 4 blini pans or 1 skillet, melt gently, then add the egg mixture.

Cook over gentle heat for about 6–8 minutes, then flip the tortilla or transfer to a preheated broiler to set and lightly brown the surface. If making a large tortilla, you should cook it for about 10 minutes before broiling.

Let cool a little, then serve topped with smoked salmon, salmon caviar, and crème fraîche.

Traditionally, pan bagnat, from Nice in the south of France, is made in a large baguette, but I prefer to use Italian ciabatta rolls. The tortilla is just one way of serving smoked salmon and eggs for brunch—I like to cook individual tortillas in little blini pans (sold in good cookware stores), but the dish is equally good cooked in a large skillet and cut into wedges.

salads, soups, and appetizers

Outdoor eating is such a joy in itself that the food needs to be very simple— just a few fresh ingredients combined to make both the meal and the experience that little bit better.

Salads, appetizers, and soups can make a whole meal just by themselves. A chilled soup is perfect in summer and a lovely way to start a meal. Remember that a thermos will keep cold soups cold as well as hot ones hot, so what better way to transport it to a picnic? Take along a few big coffee mugs or even paper cups and soup iş the easiest dish in the world to serve. If you're using a thermos, rinse it out with boiling water first if you're using it for hot foods—or with ice cubes and ice water if you're using it for cold foods.

Whatever else you serve outdoors, I think you should serve a salad, too. Sometimes it can be a course in itself: sometimes it accompanies other dishes. Keep the leaves rolled up in a cloth in the refrigerator or in a cooler and they'll stay crisp until you serve them.

My favorite appetizers include the fresh, spicy taste of East and Southeast Asian foods, as well as the strong impact of Italian foods. In fact, I think I prefer these flavors pretty well any time.

summer vegetables
with bagna cauda

Put the bagna cauda—the "hot bath"—of warm anchovy butter in the center of the table with a basket of fresh summer vegetables, so everyone can just help themselves.

8 oz. for each serving of fresh, young, summer vegetables, washed and trimmed, such as baby carrots, baby fennel bulbs, radishes, cherry tomatoes, and baby zucchini

Bagna cauda

4 tablespoons unsalted butter

3–4 large garlic cloves, crushed

2 oz. canned anchovies in oil, drained and chopped

¾ cup extra virgin olive oil

Serves 4–6

Arrange the trimmed vegetables in a basket or on a large platter.

To make the bagna cauda, put the butter and garlic into a small saucepan and heat gently. Simmer very slowly for 4–5 minutes until the garlic has softened, but not browned. Add the anchovies, stir well, then pour in the oil. Cook gently for a further 10 minutes, stirring occasionally, until the sauce is soft and almost creamy.

Transfer the sauce to a dish and serve at once with the selection of trimmed vegetables.

summer leaf and herb **salad**

inner leaves from 2 large romaine lettuces

8 oz. mixed salad leaves, such as radicchio, mâche (lamb's lettuce or corn salad), mizuna, or endive

a handful of mixed, fresh soft-leaf herbs such as basil, chives, dill, and mint

Honey lemon dressing

1 garlic clove, crushed

½ cup extra virgin olive oil

1 tablespoon lemon juice

1 teaspoon honey

1 teaspoon Dijon mustard

salt and freshly ground black pepper

Serves 4

There are thousands of recipes for simple green salads, so what makes one better than the next? I think it's just a matter of taste, and this version is one of my favorites.

Put the dressing ingredients into a bowl or small pitcher and set aside to infuse for at least 1 hour. Just before serving, strain out the garlic.

Wash the leaves, spin dry in a salad spinner (or pat dry with paper towels), and transfer to a plastic bag. Chill for 30 minutes to make the leaves crisp.

Put the leaves and herbs into a large bowl, add a little of the dressing, and toss well to coat evenly. Add a little more dressing to taste, then serve.

fava bean salad
with mint and parmesan

1–1½ lb. podded, young fresh or frozen fava beans

3 Belgian endives

leaves from 3 sprigs of mint

¼ cup freshly grated Parmesan cheese

salt

Hazelnut oil dressing

2 tablespoons extra virgin olive oil

¼ cup hazelnut oil*

2 teaspoons white wine vinegar

1 teaspoon Dijon mustard

¼ teaspoon sugar

salt and freshly ground black pepper

Serves 6

I like to serve this salad as as part of a tapas spread, but it can be served as an appetizer or snack, too. If it's early in the season and you have young, tender fava beans, it's not necessary to peel them after blanching. Out of season, you can use frozen fava beans or flat beans cut into 1-inch lengths.

Plunge the fava beans into a saucepan of lightly salted, boiling water, return to a boil, and simmer for 1–2 minutes. Drain and refresh the beans immediately under cold running water. Pat dry and peel away the gray-green outer skin if necessary. Put the peeled beans into a salad bowl.

Cut the endives in half lengthwise, slice thickly crosswise, then add to the beans. Add the mint leaves, tearing any large ones in half. Using a potato peeler, cut thin shavings of Parmesan over the salad.

Just before serving, put the dressing ingredients into a small pitcher, mix well, sprinkle over the salad, toss well, then serve.

*Note If hazelnut oil is difficult to find, substitute extra virgin olive oil. Always buy nut oils in small quantities and keep them in the refrigerator: they are delicate, and become rancid very quickly.

If you've never eaten a salad in a Japanese restaurant, then this will be a delightful surprise. The salad itself is a simple combination of ingredients plus two types of Japanese noodles—but it's the dressing that makes this so interesting.

japanese garden salad with noodles

Cook the noodles separately according to the instructions on the packages. Drain and set aside.

Blanch the snowpeas in lightly salted, boiling water for 1 minute. Drain, refresh under cold water, and dry well.

Wash and dry the lettuce leaves. Cut the carrot and cucumber into matchsticks and the tomatoes into wedges. Divide the noodles and salad ingredients between 6 serving bowls.

Put the dressing ingredients into a bowl, add ½ cup water, and stir well until the sugar has dissolved. Pour over the salad and serve at once.

4 oz. soba noodles

4 oz. udon noodles

8 oz. snowpeas, about 1½ cups

2 romaine lettuce hearts, leaves separated

2 carrots

1 cucumber

4 ripe tomatoes

salt

Japanese dressing

2 tablespoons Japanese soy sauce (shoyu)

1½ tablespoons sugar

1½ tablespoons rice vinegar

1 tablespoon sesame oil

Serves 6

A wonderful and unusual salad that I encountered on a recent trip to Bali. It can be served as part of a savory spread, as an accompaniment to broiled shrimp or even as a dessert.

indonesian chile
fruit salad

½ ripe pineapple

1 ripe papaya or mango

1 pomelo or pink grapefruit

2 large bananas

2 green apples

Chile dressing

¼ cup dark palm sugar or brown sugar

¼ cups lemon juice

2 tablespoons soy sauce

1–2 red chile peppers, such as serrano, seeded and finely chopped

Serves 6

To make the dressing, put the sugar, lemon juice, soy sauce, and 2 tablespoons water into a small saucepan and heat over low heat until the sugar has dissolved. Remove from the heat, add the chiles, and let cool.

Peel, core, and cut the pineapple into wedges, then chunks. Peel, seed, and dice the papaya or mango. Peel the pomelo or grapefruit, cut out the segments, and cut each segment in half. Peel and slice the bananas. Peel, core, and dice the apples.

Arrange all the fruit in a large bowl, toss gently in the dressing, then chill for about 15 minutes before serving.

pasta, squash, and feta salad
with olive dressing

1½ lb. butternut squash

1 tablespoon extra virgin olive oil

1 tablespoon chopped fresh thyme leaves

I lb. dried penne

10 oz. feta cheese, diced

10 oz. cherry tomatoes, about 2 cups, halved

¼ cup chopped fresh basil

¼ cup pumpkin seeds, pan-toasted in a dry skillet

salt and freshly ground black pepper

Dressing

½ cup extra virgin olive oil

3 tablespoons tapenade (see recipe introduction)

juice of 1 lemon

1 teaspoon honey

salt and freshly ground black pepper

Serves 6

Ready-made tapenade is available in supermarkets and gourmet stores and is usually quite good quality. Some stores make their own and these are definitely worth seeking out for this dish.

Peel and seed the butternut squash and cut the flesh into bite-size pieces. Put into a bowl or plastic bag, then add the oil, thyme, salt, and pepper, Toss well, then arrange in a single layer in a roasting pan. Roast in a preheated oven at 400°F for 25 minutes, or until golden and tender. Let cool.

To make the dressing, put the olive oil, tapenade, lemon juice, and honey into a bowl. Beat well, then add salt and pepper to taste.

Bring a large saucepan of lightly salted water to a boil, add the penne, and cook for about 10 minutes until *al dente* (just cooked but still slightly crunchy in the middle). Drain well, then immediately stir in ¼ cup of the dressing. Let cool.

When cool, put the pasta and squash into a salad bowl, mix gently, then add the feta cheese, cherry tomatoes, basil, and toasted pumpkin seeds. Just before serving, stir in the remaining dressing.

chicken salad with radicchio and pine nuts

I love this salad, with its rich, almost plum-like flavors of raisins and Marsala. Sherry vinegar, one of the most delicious vinegars, is sold in larger supermarkets or gourmet stores. If you can't find it, use balsamic instead.

1 small red onion, sliced

1½ lb. cooked chicken breast

1 head of radicchio, shredded

4 oz. arugula

a few sprigs of flat-leaf parsley

Marsala raisin dressing

⅓ cup extra virgin olive oil

½ cup pine nuts

½ cup raisins

2 tablespoons Marsala wine

2 tablespoons sherry vinegar

salt and freshly ground black pepper

Serves 4–6

Put the onion slices into a small bowl and cover with cold water. Let soak for 30 minutes, drain well, then dry thoroughly with paper towels.

Tear or slice the chicken into thin strips and put into a large salad bowl. Add the radicchio, arugula (leaves torn if large), parsley, and onion.

To make the dressing, put 2 tablespoons of the oil into a skillet, heat gently, add the pine nuts and raisins, and sauté for 3–4 minutes until the pine nuts are lightly golden. Add the Marsala and vinegar, with salt and pepper to taste, and let warm through. Stir in the remaining oil and remove from the heat.

Pour the dressing over the salad, toss lightly, and serve.

fresh oysters with thai dressing

Oysters are an essential outdoor experience, preferably eaten as close to the sea as you can get. Purists would never serve their oysters any way but naked (the oysters, that is), but I like to experiment with different dressings for new taste sensations.

To make the dressing, put the lemongrass, lime leaves, fish sauce, lime juice, mirin, and sugar into a blender, then add 2 tablespoons water. Blend well, then set aside to infuse for 2 hours. Strain into a clean bowl and stir in the cucumber and cilantro.

Shuck the oysters, reserving as much of the oyster liquor as possible. Spoon the dressing over the oysters and serve at once on a bed of ice.

24 fresh oysters

ice cubes, to serve

Thai dressing

1 stalk of lemongrass, very finely sliced

2 kaffir lime leaves, very finely sliced, or finely grated zest of 1 lime

2 tablespoons Thai fish sauce (*nam pla*)

1½ tablespoons lime juice

1½ tablespoons mirin (sweetened Japanese rice wine)

1 teaspoon sugar

¼ cucumber, peeled and diced

a few cilantro leaves

Serves 4

*Since moving to Sydney, I have become a real
fan of Japanese food, partly for its simplicity
but mainly for its freshness. To make this
dish, the tuna you buy must be extremely
fresh, so tell your fish seller that you will be
serving the fish as sashimi.*

tuna sashimi with pickled ginger dressing

10 oz. tuna fillet, in one piece
a few salad leaves

Pickled ginger dressing
2 tablespoons Japanese soy sauce (shoyu)
2 tablespoons rice wine vinegar
½ tablespoon sesame oil
½ tablespoon sugar
2 tablespoons sliced pickled ginger
1 tablespoon chopped fresh cilantro
a little cracked Szechuan pepper or black pepper

Serves 6

Slice the tuna very thinly and arrange on plates.

Put all the dressing ingredients into a bowl or small
pitcher, add 2 tablespoons water, and mix well.

Sprinkle over the tuna, top with a few salad leaves, and
serve at once.

three **salsas**

Salsas give an extra dimension to chicken, meat, and fish and are incredibly versatile. The hot pineapple and papaya salsa is good with shrimp or pork, the creamy corn salsa marries well with chicken, while the tomato and ginger salsa is very good with white fish or tortilla chips.

creamy corn **salsa**

1 ear of fresh corn, husk removed

2 red chile peppers, such as serrano

1 tomato, diced

1 garlic clove, crushed

juice of ½ lime

1 tablespoon maple syrup

2 tablespoons sour cream

salt and freshly ground black pepper

Serves 6

Preheat an outdoor grill or broiler until hot. Add the corn and cook for about 15 minutes, turning frequently, until charred on all sides. Let cool.

Add the chile peppers and broil until the skins are charred all over. Transfer to a bowl and cover with a clean cloth until cool.

Using a sharp knife, cut down all sides of the corn cob to remove the kernels. Put them into a bowl. Peel and seed the chile peppers, chop the flesh, then add to the corn.

Stir in all the remaining ingredients, season to taste, then serve.

hot pineapple and papaya **salsa**

½ ripe pineapple

½ large papaya

juice of 1 lime

1–2 green chile peppers, such as serrano, seeded and chopped

2 scallions, finely chopped

1 tablespoon chopped fresh mint

1 tablespoon Thai fish sauce (*nam pla*)

Serves 6

Peel the pineapple, remove and discard the core, then dice the flesh and put into a serving bowl, together with any juice.

Peel the papaya, scoop out the seeds, and dice the flesh. Add to the pineapple.

Stir in the scallions, mint, and fish sauce, set aside to infuse for about 30 minutes, then serve.

tomato, sesame, and ginger **salsa**

2 ripe tomatoes, peeled, seeded, and diced

½ red onion, finely chopped

2 inches fresh ginger, peeled and grated

1 garlic clove, chopped

1 tablespoon chopped fresh cilantro

2 tablespoons peanut oil

1 tablespoon soy sauce

1 teaspoon sesame oil

Serves 6

Put all the ingredients into a bowl, set aside to infuse for about 30 minutes, then serve.

On a hot summer's day, chilled soup is the perfect lunch dish. Melon with Parma ham is a classic Italian antipasto and is the basis of one of these delicious cold soups. The coconut soup is based on a Thai original—the contrast with the hot, aromatic garlic shrimp is just magical.

chilled coconut soup
with sizzling shrimp

2 cups coconut milk

1¼ cups plain yogurt

1 cucumber, peeled and chopped

2 tablespoons chopped fresh mint

2 tablespoons extra virgin olive oil

2 garlic cloves, thinly sliced

½ teaspoon cumin seeds

a pinch of hot red pepper flakes

8–12 uncooked jumbo shrimp, peeled and deveined

salt and freshly ground black pepper

Serves 4

Put the coconut milk, yogurt, cucumber, and mint into a blender or food processor and blend to a purée. Add salt and pepper to taste. Chill for 1 hour.

Ladle the soup into 4 bowls just before starting to cook the shrimp.

Put the oil into a large skillet and heat gently. Add the garlic, cumin seeds, and pepper flakes, and sauté very gently until the garlic is softened, but not golden. Using a slotted spoon, transfer the garlic to a small plate.

Increase the heat and add the shrimp to the skillet. Stir-fry for about 3–4 minutes until cooked through. Return the garlic mixture to the skillet, stir quickly, then immediately spoon the sizzling hot shrimp onto the soup and serve.

chilled melon soup
with serrano ham

4 cantaloupe melons

6 scallions, finely chopped

2 tablespoons chopped fresh basil

½ tablespoon ground ginger

1¼ cups plain yogurt

2 tablespoons dry sherry

2 large slices serrano ham or prosciutto

salt and freshly ground black pepper

ice cubes, to serve

Serves 4

Cut the melons in half and discard the seeds. Scoop out all the flesh and transfer it to a blender. Add the scallions and basil and blend until smooth.

Add in the ginger, yogurt, and sherry, blend until very smooth, and add salt and pepper to taste. Chill for about 1 hour.

Cook the ham under a preheated broiler until very crisp and golden. Cool and break into bite-size pieces.

Pour the soup into chilled bowls or mugs, add a few ice cubes, a sprinkling of crispy ham, and a good grinding of black pepper, then serve.

This is just one of those dishes that, once tasted, never forgotten. Pappa al pomodoro is a Tuscan "soup," although traditionally it is so thick you can almost eat it with a fork! This is my version— slightly more soup-like.

pappa al pomodoro

Put the tomatoes into a saucepan, add the stock, sugar, 2 tablespoons of the oil, and the leaves from the oregano and basil. Add a little salt and pepper, then heat slowly to boiling point. Reduce the heat, cover, and simmer gently for 30 minutes.

Toast the bread over a preheated medium-hot outdoor grill or on a stove-top grill pan until charred. Rub the bread all over with the garlic, then transfer to a plate. Sprinkle with the remaining oil and, using a fork, mash well into the bread, breaking it into small bits.

Add the bread to the soup and stir over low heat for about 5 minutes until the bread has been evenly incorporated and the soup thickened.

Add salt and freshly ground black pepper to taste and serve hot, topped with a little grated Parmesan. This dish is also delicious served cold.

2 lb. ripe red tomatoes, preferably on the vine, chopped

1¼ cups vegetable stock

1 teaspoon sugar

⅓ cup extra virgin olive oil

4 sprigs of oregano

4 sprigs of basil

4 slices dried bread, without crusts

2 garlic cloves

salt and freshly ground black pepper

freshly grated Parmesan cheese, to serve

Serves 4

vegetables and vegetarian dishes

Summer is prime vegetable-growing season, so it's no wonder this is the time when we can indulge ourselves in the ripest, reddest tomatoes, the crispest shoots of asparagus, the juiciest leaves of salads and herbs. Pick them in their prime (if you're lucky enough to have your own garden) or shop at a market that takes pride in the quality of its produce—and you can be sure of the finest flavor and quality.

You don't have to be a vegetarian to appreciate delicious vegetable dishes. In fact, even if you're doing a serious meat-lover's barbecue, you'll need lots of delicious vegetable accompaniments to serve with the entrée. I love to cook vegetables on an outdoor grill, then serve them on a large platter with a large bowl of unctuous mayonnaise for dipping, and then have everyone help themselves.

They're equally good turned into an entrée in their own right: think of vegetable-based tarts and quiches, pita breads or picnic loaves stuffed with juicy vegetables and sauces such as pesto. Vegetable pasta, frittata, and risotto are all substantial enough to become the main event for lunch in the backyard on a hot summer's day when you feel like something light.

grilled corn
with chile-salt rub

One of the Southwest's most popular chiles is the ancho, the dried version of the poblano. When ground to a fine powder, it has a smoky flavor and is mild to medium on the heat scale—delicious with the sweet, nutty taste of corn.

6 ears of corn,
husks removed

2 tablespoons extra virgin
olive oil, plus extra to serve

3 ancho peppers

1½ tablespoons salt,
preferably sea salt, plus
extra for cooking the corn

3 limes, cut into wedges

Serves 6

Trim the ends of the corn. Bring a large saucepan of lightly salted water to a boil, add the corn, and boil for 5 minutes. Drain and refresh under cold water. Pat dry.

Preheat an outdoor grill or broiler until hot. Brush the corn with oil and cook on the grill or under the broiler for 6–8 minutes, turning frequently until charred all over.

Meanwhile, remove the stalk and seeds from the dried chile peppers. Chop the flesh coarsely and, using a spice grinder or mortar and pestle, grind to a powder. Transfer to a small bowl, then mix in the salt.

Rub the lime wedges vigorously over the corn, sprinkle with the chile salt, and serve with extra oil for drizzling.

grilled artichokes
with chile-lime mayonnaise

Try to find small or baby artichokes for this dish so that they can be cooked straight on the grill without any blanching first.

18 small artichokes

1 lemon, halved

2 tablespoons extra virgin olive oil

salt and freshly ground black pepper

lime wedges, to serve

Chile-lime mayonnaise

1 chipotle chile pepper

2 egg yolks

1¼ cups olive oil

juice of 1 lime

salt, preferably sea salt

Serves 6

To make the mayonnaise, cover the chipotle with boiling water and let soak for 30 minutes. Drain and pat dry, then cut in half and scrape out the seeds.

Finely chop the flesh and put into a food processor. Add the egg yolks and a little salt and blend briefly until frothy. With the blade running, gradually pour the oil through the funnel until the sauce is thick and glossy. Add the lime juice and, if the mayonnaise is too thick, a tablespoon of warm water. Taste and adjust the seasoning, then cover and set aside.

Trim the stalks from the artichokes and cut off the top 1 inch of the globes. Slice the globes in half lengthwise, cutting out the central "choke" if necessary. Rub the cut surfaces all over with lemon juice to stop them discoloring.

Toss the artichokes with the oil and a little salt and pepper. Cook over medium-hot coals for 15–20 minutes, depending on size, until charred and tender, turning halfway through the cooking time. Serve with the mayonnaise and wedges of lime.

slow-roasted tomatoes
with ricotta and spaghetti

A pasta dish packed full of the flavors of the Mediterranean—garlic, tomatoes, oregano, and ricotta. Roast the tomatoes ahead of time if you like and then reheat at 350°F for 15 minutes.

6 large, ripe tomatoes

4 sprigs of oregano, plus 2 tablespoons chopped fresh oregano

½ cup extra virgin olive oil

1 lb. spaghetti

4 garlic cloves, sliced

1 dried red chile pepper, such as ancho or New Mexico, chopped

juice of ½ lemon

1 cup fresh ricotta cheese, crumbled into big pieces

salt and freshly ground black pepper

freshly grated Parmesan, to serve

Serves 4

Cut the tomatoes in half and arrange, cut side up, in a shallow roasting pan. Sprinkle with the sprigs of oregano, 1 tablespoon of the oil, and lots of salt and pepper.

Roast in a preheated oven at 500°F for 20 minutes. Reduce to 300°F and cook for a further 1–1½ hours until the tomatoes are golden, glossy, and reduced in size by about one-third. Remove from the oven and keep them warm.

Bring a large saucepan of lightly salted water to a boil, add the spaghetti, then return to a boil and cook for about 10 minutes, until the pasta is *al dente* (just cooked, but still slightly crunchy in the middle).

After about 5 minutes, put the remaining oil into a large, deep skillet, heat well, add the garlic, and sauté gently for 2 minutes until softened but not golden. Add the chile pepper and cook for a further minute.

Drain the cooked pasta, reserving ¼ cup of the cooking liquid. Add the pasta and reserved water to the skillet, then add the chopped oregano, lemon juice, salt and pepper. Toss over the heat for about 2 minutes.

Transfer to plates and serve topped with the tomatoes and ricotta and a light dusting of grated Parmesan.

4 tablespoons butter

1 large onion, finely chopped

2 garlic cloves, crushed

1 leek, trimmed and sliced

1½ cups arborio rice

½ cup dry vermouth or fino sherry

1 quart vegetable stock

2¼ cups fresh or frozen peas

4 oz. romaine lettuce leaves, washed and shredded

¼ cup chopped fresh mint, plus a handful of mint leaves, to serve

¼ cup mascarpone cheese

¾ cup freshly grated Parmesan cheese

salt and freshly ground black pepper

Serves 4–6

Although this risotto is best made with fresh peas, you can also use frozen. The mint adds a delicious fresh flavor. This will serve four as an entrée or six as an appetizer.

fresh pea and lettuce **risotto**

Put the butter into a saucepan, melt gently, then add the onion, garlic, and leek, and sauté gently for 10 minutes until softened but not golden. Add the rice, stir for 1 minute until all the grains are glossy, then add the vermouth or sherry. Let bubble and evaporate.

Meanwhile, put the stock into a separate saucepan and heat until just barely simmering. Add about ½ cup of the hot vegetable stock to the rice. Add the peas and a little salt and pepper, then stir until the liquid has been absorbed. Continue adding the stock and stirring the rice until almost all the stock has been used. Add the lettuce, chopped mint, and the remaining stock and cook until absorbed.

Remove from the heat, stir in the mascarpone and ¼ cup of the Parmesan, and season to taste. Cover the pan and set aside for 5 minutes before serving, topped with the remaining Parmesan and mint leaves.

With its lovely, earthy flavors, a frittata is an Italian version of the Spanish tortilla or the French omelette and different ingredients are added depending on the region or season.

mixed mushroom **frittata**

3 tablespoons extra virgin olive oil

2 shallots, finely chopped

2 garlic cloves, finely chopped

1 tablespoon chopped fresh thyme leaves

3 cups mixed wild and cultivated mushrooms, such as chanterelle, portobello, shiitake, and white button mushrooms

6 eggs

2 tablespoons chopped, fresh flat-leaf parsley

salt and freshly ground black pepper

Serves 6

Put 2 tablespoons of the oil into a nonstick skillet, heat gently, then add the shallots, garlic, and thyme. Sauté gently for 5 minutes until softened but not browned.

Meanwhile, brush off any dirt clinging to the mushrooms and wipe the caps. Chop or slice coarsely and add to the skillet. Sauté for 4–5 minutes until just starting to release their juices. Remove from the heat.

Put the eggs into a bowl with the parsley and a little salt and pepper, beat briefly, then stir in the mushroom mixture. Wipe the skillet clean.

Heat the remaining tablespoon of oil in the clean skillet and pour in the egg and mushroom mixture. Cook over medium heat for 8–10 minutes until set on the bottom. Transfer to a preheated broiler and cook for 2–3 minutes until the top is set and spotted brown. Cool and serve at room temperature.

roquefort and walnut tart

Blue cheese imparts a wonderful richness of flavor to this light, creamy tart with walnut crust. I like to serve it with salad made from arugula, pears, and walnuts as an appetizer.

To make the pastry crust, put the walnuts into a dry skillet and cook for 1–2 minutes until they start to smell toasted. Transfer to a bowl and let cool. When cool, transfer to a food processor or blender and grind to a meal. Sift the flour and salt into a bowl and rub in the butter until the mixture resembles fine bread crumbs. Stir in the ground walnuts and then enough cold water to form a soft dough, 1–2 tablespoons. Transfer the dough to a lightly floured surface, knead gently, then shape into a flat disk. Wrap in plastic wrap and chill for about 30 minutes.

Transfer the dough to a lightly floured surface, roll out to a disk about 12 inches in diameter and use to line the tart pan. Prick the bottom with a fork and chill for a further 30 minutes. Remove from the refrigerator and line the pastry crust with parchment paper and baking beans or rice. Bake in a preheated oven at 400°F for 10 minutes. Remove the paper and beans or rice and bake for a further 5–6 minutes until the crust is crisp and lightly golden. Remove from the oven and let cool for about 10 minutes.

Meanwhile, to prepare the filling, dice the Roquefort and put into a food processor. Add the ricotta, cream, eggs, walnut oil, salt, and pepper and blend briefly until mixed but not smooth. Pour into the pastry crust and cook for about 20 minutes until risen and golden. Let cool slightly in the pan, then serve warm with the salad.

To make the salad, put the walnuts into a dry frying pan, toast until golden, then remove, cool and chop coarsely. Peel, core, and slice the pears and put into a bowl. Add the arugula, parsley, and walnuts. Put the walnut oil into a measuring cup, add the olive oil, sherry vinegar, honey, salt, and pepper and beat well. Pour over the salad, toss gently, then serve with the tart.

¼ cup walnuts
½ cup all-purpose flour
1 teaspoon salt
¼ cup butter, diced

Roquefort filling

½ cup Roquefort cheese
1 cup ricotta cheese
½ cup heavy cream
3 eggs, lightly beaten
2 tablespoons walnut oil
salt and pepper

Arugula salad

½ cup walnuts
2 ripe pears
8 oz. arugula
a handful of parsley
¼ cup walnut oil
2 tablespoons olive oil
2 teaspoons sherry vinegar
1 teaspoon honey
salt and pepper

*9-inch tart pan, buttered
parchment paper
baking beans or raw rice*

Serves 6

What is it about caramelized onions? They smell just divine, especially when cooked in butter. These simple onion tarts, topped with creamy goat cheese, are best served warm, although they are also good cold.

onion, thyme, and goat cheese **tarts**

3½ tablespoons butter

1 lb. onions, finely sliced

2 garlic cloves, crushed

1 tablespoon chopped fresh thyme

¾ lb. puff pastry dough, defrosted if frozen

all-purpose flour, for rolling out

8 oz. log goat cheese

salt and freshly ground black pepper

Makes 8

Put the butter into a skillet, let melt over low heat, then add the onions, garlic, and thyme, and sauté gently for 20–25 minutes, until softened and golden. Let cool.

Put the dough onto a lightly floured surface and roll out to form a rectangle, 8 x 6 inches, trimming the edges. Cut the rectangle in half lengthwise and into 4 crosswise, making 8 pieces, about 4 inches square.

Divide the onion mixture between the squares, spreading it over the top, leaving a thin border around the edges. Cut the cheese into 8 slices and arrange in the center of each square.

Transfer the squares to a large baking tray and bake in a preheated oven at 425°F for about 12–15 minutes until the pastry has risen and the cheese is golden. Let cool a little, then serve warm.

turkish **pizza turnover**

This is similar to the Italian "calzone" or stuffed pizza. I first came across it in Sydney at a local food market. At one stall, Turkish chefs were busily kneading, rolling, and cooking these quite delicious pizzas, which were then cut into strips and served on napkins.

Sift the flour into the bowl of an electric mixer* with dough hook attached. Stir in the yeast and salt. Add the oil and ½–⅔ cup warm water and work to a dough. Transfer to a floured surface and knead for 10 minutes until the dough is smooth and elastic.

Meanwhile, to make the filling, discard any thick spinach stalks, then wash the leaves in a colander. Drain, transfer to a large saucepan, and heat gently for 2–3 minutes until the leaves have wilted. Rinse under cold water, drain completely, and squeeze out as much water as possible. Finely chop the spinach and set aside.

Heat the oil in a skillet, add the onion and garlic, and sauté gently for 5 minutes until very soft and lightly golden. Stir in the spinach, the 2 cheeses, nutmeg, and pepper, then remove from the heat.

Transfer the dough back onto a floured surface and knead it gently. Divide the dough into 4 equal pieces and roll out each piece to a rectangle 8 x 16 inches (it will be very thin). Spread a quarter of the spinach mixture over half the dough, fold over, and seal the edges. Repeat with the other pieces of dough to make 4 turnovers.

Heat the flat plate of an outdoor grill for 5 minutes, then reduce the heat to medium. Brush with a little oil, add the stuffed pizzas, and cook for about 4–5 minutes on each side until golden. Alternatively, if you don't have a grill, cook on a flat griddle or large, heavy skillet. Serve hot.

*Note If you don't have an electric mixer, use a food processor with the plastic blade attachment, or make by hand in a large mixing bowl. Gradually work the mixture together with your hands to form a soft dough, then invert onto a lightly floured surface and knead for 8–10 minutes until the dough becomes smooth and elastic.

3 cups bread flour, plus extra for kneading

1½ teaspoons active dry yeast

1½ teaspoons salt

1 tablespoon extra virgin olive oil

Cheese and spinach filling

1 lb. spinach leaves

1 tablespoon extra virgin olive oil

1 small onion, finely chopped

2 garlic cloves, crushed

4 oz. feta cheese, crumbled

2 tablespoons grated Parmesan cheese

2 tablespoons mascarpone cheese

a little grated nutmeg

freshly ground black pepper

Serves 4

beet hummus
with pan-grilled bread

Beet hummus is a delicious summery dip for vegetables or toasted bread. Cooking bread on the grill or a ridged stove-top grill pan is easy and very like the traditional way that pita bread is cooked.

8 oz. cooked beets in natural juices, drained and chopped

½ cup white bread crumbs

1 garlic clove, crushed

3 tablespoons extra virgin olive oil

2 tablespoons grated horseradish

1 tablespoon freshly squeezed lemon juice

salt and freshly ground black pepper

Bread

2 ¼ cups bread flour, plus extra for kneading

1 teaspoon sea salt

1 teaspoon active dry yeast

1 tablespoon olive oil, plus extra for oiling the bowl

Serves 6

To make the bread dough, sift the flour into the bowl of an electric mixer* with the dough hook attached. Stir in the salt and yeast, then gradually work in ⅓ cup warm water and the oil to make a soft dough. Transfer to a lightly floured surface and knead for about 8–10 minutes until smooth and elastic.

Put the dough into an oiled bowl, cover with plastic wrap, and let rise in a warm place for 45 minutes or until doubled in size.

Meanwhile, to make the hummus, put the beets, breadcrumbs, oil, horseradish, and lemon juice into a food processor, blend to a smooth purée, and season with salt and pepper to taste.

Transfer the dough to a lightly floured surface and knead it gently. Divide into 6 pieces and roll out each one to an oval, about the size of a pita bread. Cook the bread over medium-hot coals or on a ridged stove-top grill pan for 1–2 minutes on each side. Serve warm with the hummus.

*Note If you don't have an electric mixer, use a food processor with the plastic blade attachment, or make by hand in a large mixing bowl. Gradually work the mixture together with your hands to form a soft dough, then invert onto a lightly floured surface and knead for 8–10 minutes until the dough becomes smooth and elastic.

focaccia topped with cherry tomatoes and pesto

The secret to making focaccia is to let the dough rise three times rather than twice, as for regular bread dough. It is well worth the extra 30 minutes needed, as the result is light, airy, and totally delicious!

0.6 oz. cake compressed yeast or ¼ oz. package active dry yeast

a pinch of sugar

3 cups all-purpose flour, plus extra for kneading

1 tablespoon salt, preferably sea salt, plus extra for cooking

2 tablespoons extra virgin olive oil, plus extra for sprinkling

6 oz. cherry tomatoes, about 1½ cups, halved

¼ cup pitted black olives, such as niçoise, halved

Pesto

1 cup basil leaves

1 garlic clove, crushed

2 tablespoons pine nuts

⅓ cup extra virgin olive oil

2 tablespoons freshly grated Parmesan cheese

salt and freshly ground black pepper

a baking pan, 8 x 12 inches

Serves 8

Put the yeast into a small bowl, add the sugar and ¾ cup. warm water, and stir until the yeast has dissolved. Add 2 tablespoons of the flour and put in a warm place for 10 minutes until frothy.

Sift the remaining flour and the 1 tablespoon salt into the bowl of an electric mixer fitted with a dough hook and add the frothed yeast mixture and oil. Mix for about 10 minutes until smooth and elastic. Shape into a ball, transfer to an oiled bowl, cover with plastic wrap, and let rise for 1 hour or until doubled in size.

Transfer the dough to a lightly floured surface, knead gently, then shape or roll into a rectangle to fit snugly into the baking pan. Cover and let rise for 30 minutes.

Using your fingers, press indentations all over the surface of the dough. Cover again and let rise for a further 1 hour until well risen.

Meanwhile, to make the pesto, put the basil leaves, garlic, pine nuts, and olive oil into a food processor and purée to form a vivid green paste. Transfer to a bowl and stir in the cheese and salt and pepper to taste.

Spread 2–3 tablespoons of the pesto* carefully over the risen dough without letting it collapse. Add the tomatoes and olives and sprinkle with a little more oil and about ½ tablespoon salt. Bake in a preheated oven at 400°F for about 25 minutes until risen and golden. Cool on a wire rack and serve warm.

*Note Store the remaining pesto in an airtight container in the refrigerator for up to 3 days and use as a pasta sauce or in the Stuffed Picnic Loaf, page 68.

stuffed **picnic loaf**

Great for a picnic—a loaf packed with grilled vegetables, pesto, and goat cheese. Make it a day ahead so it can be "pressed" overnight in the refrigerator for the flavors to develop and mingle.

1 round loaf of bread, about 9 inches diameter, 4 inches high

2 tablespoons extra virgin olive oil

½ quantity pesto (page 67)

2 large red onions

2 large red bell peppers

2 large zucchini

8 oz. soft goat cheese, diced

12 large basil leaves

salt and freshly ground black pepper

Serves 6

Cut the top off the loaf and carefully scoop out most of the bread, leaving just the outer shell (reserve the bread and make into crumbs for another dish). Put 1 tablespoon of the oil into a bowl, stir in the pesto, and spread half the mixture around the inside of the shell and lid. Set aside.

Cut the onions into wedges, brush with a little of the remaining tablespoon of oil, and cook on a preheated outdoor grill or on a stove-top grill pan for 10 minutes on each side until very tender. Let cool.

Cook the peppers on the preheated grill or grill pan or under an overhead broiler for about 15 minutes until blackened all over. Transfer to a plastic bag and let cool. Peel away the skin, discard the seeds, and cut the flesh into quarters, reserving any juices.

Cut the zucchini lengthwise into 1-inch slices, brush with oil, and grill or broil as above for 2–3 minutes on each side until lightly charred and softened. Let cool.

Arrange the filling in layers inside the loaf, with the goat cheese and remaining pesto in the middle. Sprinkle with any remaining oil and the pepper juices and replace the lid.

Wrap the whole loaf in plastic wrap and put onto a plate. Top with a board and a heavy food can to weigh it down. Chill in the refrigerator overnight.

The next day, cut into wedges and serve.

fish and seafood

My favorite holiday memories are of walking along a beach or harbor and being seduced by the aromas issuing from nearby tavernas or cafés—the smell of calamari or shrimp being broiled over charcoal to be served simply dressed with a drizzle of local olive oil and a squeeze of lemon.

Cooking such delights for yourself is just as easy and no less rewarding and if you happen to be near the ocean, then even better. If you normally shy away from cooking fish and seafood indoors, then grilling outdoors is the solution. Most of the recipes in this chapter can just as easily be cooked on a grill as in a pan or in an oven, and those that do require a stove are ideal for when you are entertaining in the backyard.

Remember, summer is the time when light, healthful fish and seafood are particularly appealing. Fish markets and supermarkets see this as their prime season, so you'll find the best and freshest ingredients on sale. Shrimp and lobsters, crabs and squid, clams and mussels, wild fish and farmed—take your pick and give your guests a treat.

71

tiger shrimp with herb mayonnaise

2 lb. cooked tiger shrimp
lemon wedges, to serve

Herb mayonnaise
2 egg yolks
1 tablespoon lemon juice
1 teaspoon Dijon mustard
1¼ cups olive oil
¼ cup chopped mixed herbs,
such as basil, chives, chervil,
dill, parsley, and tarragon
salt and freshly ground
black pepper

Serves 6

Summer and picnics are all about this type of simple, delicious, messy food. Peel big, juicy, cooked shrimp, then dunk them into a bowl of wonderful homemade herb mayonnaise. Use a plain olive oil, rather than extra virgin, for mayonnaise, or it can be rather bitter.

To make the mayonnaise, put the egg yolks, lemon juice, mustard, and a little salt and pepper into a food processor and blend briefly until frothy. With the motor running, slowly pour the oil through the funnel to make a thick, glossy sauce. If it becomes too thick, thin it with a little warm water. Add the chopped herbs and blend again until the mayonnaise is a vibrant speckled green.

Peel the shrimp and serve with the mayonnaise and wedges of lemon.

Meat and fish (the old-fashioned surf 'n' turf)
can work well and this recipe is a perfect
example of this balance of strong flavors.
I use the chorizo sausage that needs cooking,
rather than the cured tapas variety, although
either would do.

shrimp, chorizo, and sage **skewers**

10 oz. uncooked chorizo

24 large, uncooked, peeled shrimp, deveined

24 large sage leaves

extra virgin olive oil

lemon juice

freshly ground black pepper

12 skewers, metal or bamboo (if using bamboo,
soak them in warm water for 30 minutes)

Serves 6

Cut the chorizo into 24 slices about ½ inch thick and
thread onto the skewers, alternating with the shrimp
and sage leaves. Put a little oil and lemon juice into
a small bowl or pitcher, mix well, then drizzle over the
skewers. Sprinkle with pepper.

Meanwhile, preheat an overhead broiler, stove-top
grill pan, or outdoor grill until hot. Cook the skewers
for 1½–2 minutes on each side until the chorizo and
shrimp are cooked through. Serve at once.

I've been a fan of coconut ever since I first fell in love with my mother's coconut pyramid cookies! These days, I'm more fascinated with the combinations found in Indonesian and Thai cooking. Seafood has a natural affinity with coconut and you'll love this combination.

lemongrass skewered scallops
with coconut dressing

24 large scallops

2 tablespoons peanut oil

grated zest of 2 limes

2 red chile peppers, such as serrano, seeded and chopped

2 teaspoons grated fresh ginger

1 garlic clove, crushed

1 tablespoon Thai fish sauce (*nam pla*)

Coconut milk dressing

⅓ cup coconut milk

1 tablespoon Thai fish sauce (*nam pla*)

2 teaspoons sugar

2 teaspoons coconut or rice wine vinegar*

6 bamboo skewers, soaked in warm water for 30 minutes

Serves 6

Trim the tough white muscle from the side of each scallop. Put the scallops into a shallow non-metal dish.

Put the peanut oil, lime zest, chile peppers, ginger, garlic, and fish sauce into a small pitcher or bowl, mix well, then pour over the scallops. Set aside to marinate in the refrigerator for 1 hour.

To make the dressing, put the coconut milk, fish sauce, sugar, and vinegar into a small saucepan, heat gently to dissolve the sugar, then bring to a gentle simmer until thickened slightly. Remove from the heat and let cool completely.

Meanwhile, preheat a broiler, stove-top grill pan, or outdoor grill until hot.

Thread the scallops onto the prepared skewers and cook for 1 minute on each side. Don't overcook or the scallops will be tough. Serve with the coconut dressing.

*Note Coconut and palm vinegar are used in Thailand and the Philippines: both are milder than regular vinegars. Buy them in Asian food stores or use white rice vinegar as an alternative.

squid piri-piri

Piri-piri, a Portuguese chile condiment traditionally used to baste broiled chicken, is a combination of chopped red chile peppers, olive oil, and vinegar. It is generally very hot and only a little is needed to add spice to the food. Here I have tempered the heat, but you can use more chiles if you like it spicier. It works very well with squid.

8 medium squid bodies, about 8 oz. each*

freshly squeezed juice of 1 lemon, plus extra lemon wedges, to serve

salt, preferably sea salt

Piri-piri sauce

8 small red chile peppers, such as bird's eye

1¼ cups extra virgin olive oil

1 tablespoon white wine vinegar

salt and freshly ground black pepper

16 bamboo skewers, soaked in warm water for 30 minutes

Serves 4

To prepare the squid, put the squid body on a board and, using a sharp knife, cut down one side and open the tube out flat. Scrape away any remaining insides and wash and dry well.

Skewer each opened-out body with 2 skewers, running them up the long sides of each piece. Rub a little salt over each one and squeeze over the lemon juice. Marinate in the refrigerator for 30 minutes.

Meanwhile, to make the piri-piri, finely chop the whole chile peppers without seeding them, and transfer to a small jar or bottle. Add the oil, vinegar, and a little salt and pepper. Shake well and set aside.

Meanwhile, preheat a broiler, stove-top grill pan, or outdoor grill until hot.

Baste the squid with a little of the piri-piri and cook for 1–1½ minutes on each side until charred. Drizzle with extra sauce and serve with lemon wedges.

*Note If the squid includes the tentacles, cut them off in one piece, thread with a skewer, and cook and marinate in the same way as the bodies.

grilled lobsters with "burnt" butter

I use just the lobster tails for this recipe. If your lobsters have claws, remember to crack them before serving. You can also cook this recipe with either langoustines or jumbo shrimp.

6 uncooked lobster tails
or 12 large langoustines
or jumbo shrimp*

2 tablespoons olive oil

1 stick butter

salt and freshly ground black
pepper

To serve
lemon wedges

green salad

Serves 6

Using a very sharp knife, cut the lobster tails in half lengthwise, cutting down through the shell. Brush the flesh with oil and season well with salt and pepper.

Preheat a stove-top grill pan or outdoor grill until medium hot. Add the lobster tails and cook, shell side down, for about 5 minutes. Brush with more oil and cook, flesh side down, for a further 3 minutes. Remove from the heat and let rest for 5 minutes.

Put the butter into a small saucepan and heat gently until melted and golden. Arrange the lobster tails on a large platter, drizzle with the butter, and squeeze the lemon wedges over the top. Serve with a little green salad.

*Note If using langoustines or shrimp, simply cut them in half and discard the vein running along the back of each one. Cook as above for 2 minutes each side until cooked through.

broiled **miso cod**

This marinade is typical of Japanese cooking and imparts a really fantastic flavor to the fish. Miso is a fermented soybean-based paste, available in Asian stores, gourmet food stores, and some larger supermarkets. As a guide, the lighter the color, the sweeter the flavor.

3 tablespoons Japanese soy sauce (shoyu)

3 tablespoons sake

3 tablespoons honey

2 tablespoons miso paste

6 cod fillets, 8 oz. each

vegetable oil, for brushing

To serve

pickled ginger

stir-fried baby bok choy

steamed rice

Serves 6

Put the soy sauce, sake, honey, and miso into a small saucepan and heat gently until smooth. Set aside to cool completely. Pour into a shallow dish, add the cod fillets, cover, and let marinate in the refrigerator for at least 4 hours.

Return to room temperature for 1 hour before cooking. Transfer the fillets to a broiler pan lined with foil. Cook under a preheated broiler for 4 minutes on each side, basting halfway through. Let rest for 5 minutes, then serve with pickled ginger, bok choy, and rice.

grilled fish bathed in oregano and lemon

I have many fond memories of summer holidays in Greece—and none is more prized than the smell of seafood emanating from the dozens of little tavernas dotted along the beach. This is a typical dish of char-grilled bream with oil, oregano, and garlic, but you could use other small fish such as snapper, or even trout.

2 lemons

1 cup extra virgin olive oil

1 tablespoon dried oregano

2 garlic cloves,
finely chopped

2 tablespoons chopped
fresh flat-leaf parsley

6 snapper or bream, about
12 oz. each, well cleaned
and scaled

salt and freshly ground
black pepper

Serves 6

Grate the zest of 1 lemon into a small bowl and squeeze in the juice. Add ¾ cup of the oil, the oregano, garlic, parsley, salt, and pepper. Let it infuse for at least 1 hour.

Wash and dry the fish inside and out. Using a sharp knife, cut several slashes into each side. Squeeze the juice from the remaining lemon into a bowl, add the remaining ¼ cup of oil, salt, and pepper and rub the mixture all over the fish.

Heat the flat plate of an outdoor grill for 10 minutes, add the fish, and cook for 3–4 minutes on each side until charred and cooked through. Alternatively, use a large, heavy skillet or stove-top grill pan. Transfer to a large, warm platter, pour over the dressing, and let rest for 5 minutes before serving.

A great way to prepare whole salmon is to remove the central bone from the fish, then tie the two fillets back together. If your filleting skills are limited, just ask your friendly fish seller to fillet the whole fish for you.

whole salmon stuffed with herbs

Put the salmon fillets flat onto a board, flesh side up. Carefully pull out any remaining bones with tweezers.

Put the butter, herbs, lemon zest, garlic, and plenty of pepper into a small bowl and beat well. Spread the mixture over one of the salmon fillets and put the second on the top, arranging them top to tail.

Using kitchen twine, tie the fish together at 1-inch intervals. Brush with a little oil, sprinkle with salt and freshly ground black pepper, and cook on the flat plate of an outdoor grill for 10 minutes on each side. Let rest for a further 10 minutes. Remove the twine and serve the fish cut into portions.

4 lb. whole salmon, filleted

1 stick butter, softened

1 cup chopped, fresh soft-leaf mixed herbs, such as basil, chives, mint, parsley, and tarragon

grated zest of 1 lemon

1 garlic clove, crushed

salt and freshly ground black pepper

olive oil, for brushing

Serves 8

peppered tuna steak
with salsa rossa

Salsa rossa is one of those divine Italian sauces that transforms simple meat and fish dishes into food nirvana. The slight sweetness from the peppers is a good foil for the spicy pepper crust.

⅓ cup mixed peppercorns, coarsely crushed

6 tuna steaks, 8 oz. each

1 tablespoon extra virgin olive oil

salad leaves, to serve

Salsa rossa

1 large red bell pepper

1 tablespoon extra virgin olive oil

2 garlic cloves, crushed

2 large ripe tomatoes, peeled and coarsely chopped

a small pinch of hot red pepper flakes

1 tablespoon dried oregano

1 tablespoon red wine vinegar

salt and freshly ground black pepper

Serves 6

To make the salsa rossa, broil the pepper until charred all over, then put into a plastic bag and let cool. Remove and discard the skin and seeds, reserving any juices, then chop the flesh.

Put the oil into a skillet, heat gently, then add the garlic and sauté for 3 minutes. Add the tomatoes, pepper flakes, and oregano and simmer gently for 15 minutes. Stir in the peppers and the vinegar and simmer for a further 5 minutes to evaporate any excess liquid.

Transfer to a blender and purée until fairly smooth. Add salt and pepper to taste and let cool. It may be stored in a screw-top jar in the refrigerator for up to 3 days.

Put the crushed peppercorns onto a large plate. Brush the tuna steaks with oil, then press the crushed peppercorns into the surface. Preheat a stove-top grill pan or outdoor grill until hot, add the tuna, and cook for 1 minute on each side. Wrap loosely in foil and let rest for 5 minutes before serving with the salsa rossa and a salad of mixed leaves.

meat and poultry

The outdoor grill is my favorite way of cooking meat for al fresco dining, and I like to marinate it overnight beforehand so the flavors penetrate deeply. Such age-old methods of flavoring and tenderizing meat can be found in India, the Middle East, Indonesia, Thailand, and Japan: every cuisine provides similar delicious morsels, as this chapter will show.

For the outdoor cook, skewered meats are ideal. They're easy to prepare and quick to cook (and delicious to eat). However, no recipe book for eating outdoors would be complete without the two great classics; grilled spareribs and the beef burger.

When cooking outdoors, remember that food takes longer to cook on an outdoor grill than on top of the stove or in the oven. Remove marinated foods from the refrigerator about an hour before cooking to let them return to room temperature. That way, they'll cook properly and won't be underdone in the middle. One hour before you begin cooking, start preparing the grill. If using charcoal, light the coals and heat for 40–45 minutes. The coals should have passed the red-hot phase and become lightly covered with ash before you add the food, so it will cook properly without burning on the outside.

orange and soy **glazed duck**

This is a great dish when you are short of time—it is quick to cook and tastes delicious. Serve the duck breasts with your choice of vegetables such as steamed napa cabbage, bok choy (also known as pak choi), steamed broccoli, or sautéed spinach.

4 duck breast fillets, about 8 oz. each

juice of 1 orange

3 tablespoons dark soy sauce

2 tablespoons maple syrup

½ teaspoon Chinese five-spice powder

2 garlic cloves, crushed

freshly ground Szechuan peppercorns or black pepper

To serve

steamed broccoli or bok choy, or sautéed spinach

1 orange, cut into wedges

Serves 4

Using a sharp knife, score the fat on each duck breast crosswise several times. Put the breasts into a shallow dish.

Put the orange juice, soy sauce, maple syrup, five-spice powder, garlic, and pepper into a small pitcher or bowl, mix well, then pour the mixture over the fillets. Cover with plastic wrap and marinate in the refrigerator for as long as possible. You can leave them overnight, but return them to room temperature for 1 hour before cooking.

Heat a stove-top grill pan until hot, add the duck breasts, skin side down, and sear for 1–2 minutes. Transfer to a roasting pan, adding the marinade juices. Cook the duck in a preheated oven at 400°F for about 10 minutes or until medium rare. Remove the duck from the oven, wrap it in foil, and keep it warm for 5 minutes.

Pour the juices from the roasting pan into a small saucepan and, using a large spoon, very carefully skim the fat off the surface. Transfer the pan to the top of the stove and bring the juices to a boil for 2 minutes, until thickened slightly. Serve the duck breasts sprinkled with the juices and accompanied by the broccoli, bok choy, or spinach and wedges of orange.

duck yakitori

⅓ cup Japanese soy sauce

3 tablespoons sake

2 tablespoons sugar

4 small duck breast fillets, about 5 oz. each, skinned

soba noodles, cooked according to the package instructions, then drained and chilled, to serve

Cucumber salad

2 tablespoons rice vinegar

2 tablespoons sugar

½ cucumber, about 8 inches, finely sliced

1 red chile pepper, such as serrano, seeded and chopped

8 bamboo skewers soaked in warm water for 30 minutes

Serves 4

Put the soy sauce, sake, and sugar into a small saucepan and heat gently to dissolve the sugar. Cool completely.

Cut the duck lengthwise into ⅛-inch strips and put into a shallow dish. Pour over the soy sauce mixture and marinate in the refrigerator for 2–4 hours or overnight.

Just before cooking the duck, prepare the salad. Put the vinegar, sugar, and 2 tablespoons water into a small saucepan, heat to dissolve the sugar, then let cool. Stir in the cucumber and chile and set aside.

Thread the duck strips onto skewers, zigzagging back and forth. Cook on a preheated outdoor grill or under a broiler for 2 minutes on each side until cooked through. Serve with chilled soba noodles and the cucumber salad.

chicken kabobs
moroccan-style

1 lb. chicken breast fillets, skinned

2 tablespoons extra virgin olive oil

freshly squeezed juice of 1 large lemon

1 tablespoon chopped fresh thyme leaves

2 garlic cloves, crushed

1 teaspoon ground turmeric

1 teaspoon ground cinnamon

½ teaspoon ground allspice

½ teaspoon salt

¼ teaspoon ground cayenne pepper

To serve

lemon wedges

plain yogurt

8 bamboo skewers soaked in warm water for 30 minutes

Serves 4

Cut the chicken lengthwise into ⅛-inch strips and put into a shallow, non-metal dish. Put the oil, lemon juice, thyme, garlic, turmeric, cinnamon, allspice, salt, and cayenne pepper into a pitcher, mix well, then pour over the chicken. Cover the dish and let marinate overnight in the refrigerator.

The next day, return to room temperature for 1 hour. Thread the strips onto skewers, zigzagging back and forth. Cook on a preheated outdoor grill or stove-top grill pan for 3–4 minutes on each side until charred and cooked through. Serve with lemon wedges and yogurt.

Ever since I first discovered Japanese food, I have been a huge fan, especially of the pungent flavors of skewered teriyaki and yakitori. The rich sauce copes perfectly with the gamy flavors of duck and tenderizes the flesh beautifully. The Moroccan version is, of course, the kabob, and is wondrously flavored with scented North African spices.

chicken "panini"
with mozzarella

"Panini" is the Italian word for little sandwiches, usually toasted. Here, instead of bread, we are toasting (or grilling) a chicken breast fillet stuffed with basil and mozzarella— melted, gooey, and totally delicious!

Cut the mozzarella into 8 thick slices and set aside.

Put the chicken breasts onto a board and, using a sharp knife, cut horizontally through the thickness without cutting all the way through. Open out flat and season the insides with a little salt and pepper.

Put 2 basil leaves, a few garlic slices, and 2 slices of cheese into each breast, then fold back over, pressing firmly together. Secure with toothpicks.

Brush the packages with a little oil and cook on a preheated outdoor grill or stove-top grill pan for about 8 minutes on each side until the cheese is beginning to ooze at the sides. Serve hot with the salsa rossa and sprinkle with a few basil leaves.

8 oz. mozzarella cheese

4 large, skinless, boneless chicken breasts

8 large basil leaves

2 garlic cloves, sliced thinly

1 tablespoon olive oil

salt and freshly ground black pepper

To serve

salsa rossa (page 88)

basil leaves

Serves 4

grilled mexican-style **cornish hens**

Butterflied Cornish hens are ideally suited to grilling, as the process of opening them out flat ensures quick and even cooking. The marinade ingredients have a Mexican flavor and work particularly well accompanied by the Creamy Corn Salsa on page 41.

4 Cornish game hens

creamy corn salsa, to serve
(page 41)

Mexican marinade

4 jalapeño chile peppers

8 garlic cloves, peeled

¼ cup orange juice

2 tablespoons lime juice

1 tablespoon ground cumin

1 tablespoon dried oregano
or thyme

2 teaspoons salt

⅓ cup olive oil

1 tablespoon maple syrup
or honey

Serves 4

To butterfly the hens, turn them breast side down and, using poultry shears or sturdy kitchen shears, cut down each side of the backbone and discard it. Turn the birds over and open them out flat, pressing down hard on the breastbone. Thread 2 skewers diagonally through each hen from the wings to the thigh bones.

To make the marinade, skewer the chile peppers and garlic together and cook on a preheated medium-hot outdoor grill or under a broiler for 10 minutes, turning frequently, until evenly browned. Scrape off and discard the skins from the chile peppers and chop the flesh coarsely. Put the flesh and seeds into a blender, add the garlic and all the remaining marinade ingredients, and blend to a purée.

Pour the marinade over the hens and let marinate in the refrigerator overnight. Return them to room temperature for 1 hour before cooking

When ready to cook, remove the birds from their marinade and grill over preheated medium-hot coals for 12 minutes on each side, basting occasionally. Remove from the heat, let rest for 5 minutes, then serve with the creamy corn salsa.

chicken caesar **wrap**

This salad has traveled all over the world and many additions to the basic lettuce and croutons with cheese and anchovy dressing can be found. Recently, I saw "Caesar Salad Wrap" on offer at a sandwich shop: I thought it would be a great idea for a picnic dish.

Broil or sauté the bacon for 2–3 minutes until crisp. Cool, then cut into thin strips. Shred the chicken into large strips.

To make the dressing, put the egg yolk into a small bowl, add the lemon juice, Worcestershire sauce, and a little salt and pepper and beat until frothy. Gradually beat in the oil, a little at a time, until thickened and glossy. Add 2 tablespoons water to thin the sauce, then stir in the cheese.

Lay the tortilla flat on a work surface and arrange a little lettuce down the middle of each one. Top with chicken, bacon, anchovies, a spoonful of the dressing, then, more lettuce. Wrap the tortilla into a roll, then wrap the roll in a napkin. Repeat to make 6 wraps. Serve immediately or chill to serve later.

3 large strips of bacon

8 oz. cooked chicken breast

6 small flour tortillas

1 large romaine lettuce, shredded (inner leaves only)

12 anchovy fillets in oil, drained and chopped

Caesar dressing

1 egg yolk

1 tablespoon lemon juice

1 teaspoon Worcestershire sauce

½ cup olive oil

¼ cup freshly grated Parmesan cheese

salt and freshly ground black pepper

Serves 6

tex-mex **pork rack**

2 racks barbecue spareribs, 1 lb. each

Sweet chile marinade
2 garlic cloves, crushed
2 tablespoons sea salt
2 tablespoons ground cumin
2 teaspoons chilli powder
1 teaspoon dried oregano
½ cup maple syrup or honey
¼ cup red wine vinegar
¼ cup olive oil

Serves 4–6

Wash the ribs and pat them dry with paper towels.
Transfer to a shallow, non-metal dish.

Put all the marinade ingredients into a bowl, mix well,
pour over the ribs, then work in well with your hands.
Cover and let marinate overnight in the refrigerator.

The next day, return the ribs to room temperature for
1 hour, then cook on a preheated medium-hot outdoor
grill for about 30 minutes, turning and basting
frequently with the marinade juices. Cool a little,
then serve with chile-spiked cornbread (right).

chile-spiked **cornbread**

1¼ cups medium cornmeal
1¼ cups all-purpose flour
1½ teaspoons salt
1 tablespoon baking powder
2 eggs, beaten
1 cup milk
2 tablespoons olive oil
2 large red chile peppers, such as
Anaheim or New Mexico, seeded
and chopped
1 cup canned corn kernels, drained
¼ cup finely grated Cheddar cheese
2 tablespoons chopped fresh cilantro

*a cake pan, 8 inches square,
greased and bottom-lined with
parchment paper*

Serves 8

Put the cornmeal, flour, salt, and baking powder into
a bowl and mix. Make a well in the center and pour in
the eggs, milk, and olive oil. Beat with a wooden spoon
to make a smooth batter.

Fold in the chile peppers, corn, cheese, and cilantro,
then spoon into the prepared cake pan. Bake in a
preheated oven at 400°F for 25 minutes, or until a
skewer inserted in the center comes out clean.

Remove from the oven and let cool in the pan for
about 5 minutes, then invert onto a wire rack to cool
completely. Serve cut into squares.

mini **pork and apple pies**

8 oz. pork loin, diced

4 oz. pork belly, diced

3 slices bacon, chopped

1 oz. chicken livers

1 small onion, minced

1 tablespoon chopped sage

1 small garlic clove, crushed

a pinch of ground nutmeg

1 red apple, peeled, cored, and diced

salt and black pepper

Pie crust

2½ cups all-purpose flour, plus extra for kneading

1½ teaspoons salt

¼ cup vegetable shortening

Glaze

1 egg yolk

1 tablespoon milk

1 jam jar

6 pieces of wax paper, about 12 x 3 inches

a baking sheet

Serves 6

Put the pork loin, pork belly, bacon, and chicken livers into a food processor and blend briefly to grind the meat. Transfer to a bowl and mix in the onion, sage, garlic, nutmeg, and a little salt and pepper. Set aside.

To make the pie crust, sift the flour and salt into a bowl. Put the shortening and ½ cup water into a saucepan and heat gently until the shortening melts and the water comes to a boil. Pour the liquid into the flour and, using a wooden spoon, gently draw the flour into the liquid to form a soft dough.

Let cool for a few minutes and, as soon as the dough is cool enough to handle, knead lightly in the bowl until smooth.

Divide the dough into 8 and roll out 6 of these on a lightly floured surface to form disks 5 inches across. Carefully invert them, one at a time, over an upturned jam jar. Wrap a piece of wax paper around the outside, then tie around the middle with kitchen twine.

Turn the whole thing over so the dough is sitting flat. Carefully work the jar up and out of the pie crust (you may need to slip a small spatula down between the dough and the jar, to loosen it).

Divide the pork filling into 6 portions and put 1 portion into each pie. Put the diced apple on top. Roll out the remaining 2 pieces of dough and cut 3 disks from each piece with a cookie cutter, the same size as the top of the pies.

Put a disk of dough on top of each pie, press the edges together to seal, then turn the edges inward and over to form a rim.

To make the glaze, put the egg yolk and milk into a bowl, beat well, then brush over the tops of the pies. Pierce each one with a fork to let the steam escape. Transfer to a large baking sheet and cook in a preheated oven at 375°F for 45–50 minutes until golden. Remove from the oven, transfer to a wire rack, let cool, and serve cold.

thai-style **beef salad**

1 tablespoon Szechuan peppercorns, or black peppercorns, lightly crushed

1 teaspoon ground coriander

1 teaspoon sea salt

1 lb. beef fillet, in one piece

1 tablespoon peanut or canola oil

1 cucumber, finely sliced

4 scallions, finely sliced

2 baby bok choy, finely sliced

a handful of Thai basil

a handful of mint

a handful of cilantro

Lime dressing

1 tablespoon palm sugar or brown sugar

1 tablespoon Asian fish sauce (*nam pla*)

2 tablespoons lime juice

2 small, hot red chile peppers, such as bird's eye, seeded and chopped

1 garlic clove, crushed

Serves 4

What I love about many Thai dishes (as well as Vietnamese and Indonesian) is their use of fresh herbs. Many of their salads, soups, and stews are flooded with the pungent flavors of Thai basil, mint, and cilantro. Thai basil is available from Asian stores, but you could use regular basil instead. Bok choy is also known as "pak choi" in some places.

Put the peppercorns, coriander, and salt onto a plate and mix. Rub the beef all over with the oil and then put onto the plate and turn to coat with the spices.

Cook the beef on a preheated outdoor grill or stove-top grill pan for about 10 minutes, turning to brown evenly. Remove from the heat and let cool.

Meanwhile, to make the dressing, put the sugar into a saucepan, add the fish sauce and 2 tablespoons water, and heat until the sugar dissolves. Let cool, then stir in the lime juice, chiles, and garlic.

Cut the beef into thin slices and put into a large bowl. Add the cucumber, scallions, bok choy, and herbs. Pour over the dressing, toss well, then serve.

best-ever **beef burger**

There are many burger recipes and everyone has their favorite—this one is very good. I always serve it in a bun, with pickles and sauce, and a simple salad of tomatoes, lettuce, and olives.

1 ½ lb. sirloin steak, ground*

2 oz. skinless pork belly, ground*

8 anchovy fillets in oil, drained and finely chopped

1 cup soft white bread crumbs

2 tablespoons chopped fresh thyme

1 tablespoon wholegrain mustard

1 large egg, lightly beaten

salt and freshly ground black pepper

To serve

hamburger buns

sautéed onions

dill pickles

tomato, lettuce, and olive salad (optional)

Serves 6

Put the ground steak and pork into a bowl and add the anchovies, bread crumbs, thyme, mustard, beaten egg, salt, and pepper, working it with your hands to make a nice, sticky mixture.

Shape into 6 burgers and chill for 1 hour. Cook on a preheated outdoor grill or in a lightly oiled skillet for about 4 minutes on each side. Remove from the heat and let rest for 5 minutes. Serve in a bun, with sautéed onions, dill pickles, and the tomato, lettuce, and olive salad, if using.

*Note To make the ground meat for the burger, ask your butcher to put the beef and pork through a meat grinder. Alternatively, put it into a food processor and pulse briefly to make a slightly coarse mixture.

I once worked in a London wine bar, where one of the regular dishes on the menu was a filet steak topped with a slice of blue cheese butter. It was very popular with the diners (and the staff, too)—this is my interpretation.

steak with blue cheese butter

To make the blue cheese butter, put the butter, cheese, walnuts, and parsley into a bowl and beat well. Season with salt and pepper to taste. Form into a log, wrap in foil, and chill for about 30 minutes.

Lightly season the steaks and cook on a preheated outdoor grill (or sauté in a little oil in a skillet on top of the stove) for 3 minutes on each side for rare, or 4–5 minutes for medium to well done.

Cut the butter into 8 slices. Put 2 slices of butter onto each cooked steak, wrap loosely with foil, and let rest for 5 minutes.

Serve the steaks with a salad of baby spinach.

4 top loin or tenderloin steaks, 8 oz. each

salt and freshly ground black pepper

baby spinach salad, to serve

Blue cheese butter

4 tablespoons unsalted butter, softened

2 oz. soft blue cheese, such as Gorgonzola

¼ cup walnuts, finely ground in a blender

2 tablespoons chopped fresh parsley

salt and freshly ground black pepper

Serves 4

The classic Greek kabob, called "souvlaki," is a delicious combination of cubed lamb marinated in red wine with herbs and lemon juice. The meat is tenderized by the wine, resulting in a juicy, succulent dish.

kabobs with cracked wheat salad

Trim any large pieces of fat from the lamb, then cut the meat into 1-inch cubes. Put into a shallow, non-metal dish. Add the rosemary, oregano, onion, garlic, wine, lemon juice, olive oil, salt, and pepper. Toss well, cover, and let marinate in the refrigerator for 4 hours. Return to room temperature for 1 hour before cooking.

To make the salad, soak the cracked wheat in warm water for 30 minutes until the water is absorbed and the grains have softened. Strain well to extract any excess water and transfer the wheat to a bowl. Add all the remaining ingredients, season to taste, and set aside for 30 minutes to develop the flavors.

Thread the lamb onto large rosemary stalks or metal skewers. Cook on a preheated outdoor grill or under a broiler for 10 minutes, turning and basting from time to time. Let rest for 5 minutes, then serve with the salad.

2 lb. boneless lamb, such as shoulder

1 tablespoon chopped fresh rosemary, plus 6 large stalks, for skewering, if using

1 tablespoon dried oregano

1 onion, chopped

4 garlic cloves, chopped

1¼ cups red wine

juice of 1 lemon

⅓ cup olive oil

salt and pepper

Cracked wheat salad

3¼ cups cracked wheat (bulghur wheat)

1 cup chopped fresh parsley

½ cup fresh mint leaves

2 garlic cloves, crushed

½ cup olive oil

juice of 2 lemons

a pinch of sugar

salt and pepper

6 large rosemary stalks or metal skewers

Serves 6

butterflied lamb with indian spices

"Butterfly" is the term used when a piece of meat or fish is opened out flat. When preparing a leg of lamb, the bone is removed so the meat can be laid out flat, so it will cook quickly and evenly. It's easy to do, but you can also ask your butcher to do it for you. Serve the lamb with Indian breads such as naan or chapattis, or with pita bread.

3 lb. leg of lamb, butterflied

1 onion, chopped

4 garlic cloves, chopped

1 tablespoon grated fresh ginger

1 cinnamon stick, coarsely crumbled

1 tablespoon coriander seeds

2 teaspoons cumin seeds

¼ teaspoon whole cloves

1 tablespoon curry powder

2 tablespoons tomato purée

2 tablespoons peanut or canola oil, plus extra for brushing

salt and freshly ground black pepper

To serve

Indian breads

plain yogurt

sprigs of cilantro

Serves 6–8

To butterfly the lamb, turn to the side of the leg where the bone is closest to the surface. Using a sharp knife, cut down the length of the bone, then run your knife close to the bone, using small cuts, to separate the bone from the flesh. Remove and discard the bone.

Open out the butterflied lamb and cut several shallow slashes in each side.

Put the onion, garlic, and ginger into a blender and work to a smooth paste. Transfer to a bowl.

Put the cinnamon stick, coriander and cumin seeds, and cloves into a dry skillet and heat gently until lightly browned and aromatic. Cool slightly, then grind to a powder in a spice grinder or with a mortar and pestle. Add to the onion paste, then stir in the curry powder, tomato purée, oil, salt, and pepper.

Spread this paste all over the lamb, cover, and let marinate overnight in the refrigerator. Return to room temperature for about 1 hour before cooking.

When ready to cook, scrape off the excess marinade, brush the lamb with a little oil, and put on the grill rack over medium-hot coals. Cook for 12–15 minutes on each side until the outside is charred (leaving the center beautifully pink). Remove the lamb from the heat and let it rest for 10 minutes before carving.

Serve the lamb with Indian breads, plain yogurt, and a few sprigs of cilantro.

sweet things

Summer is prime time for fruit, so who can avoid the temptation to serve it ripe and sweet and full of flavor, churned into ice creams, as toppings for desserts such as a sweet cloud of meringue, or baked into cakes or tarts?

The simplest way, of course, is in fruit salad. Make sure the fruit is ripe and good, then just sprinkle with a little sugar and perhaps liqueur and serve as it is—or perhaps with a dab of cream or a scoop of ice cream.

Chocolate is, naturally, in a class of its own—the only concern in summer is that it might melt first, before you have a chance to have it melt in your mouth. My refrigerator chocolate cake is the answer!

Most of us have a sweet tooth and perhaps it's even sweeter when indulged outdoors. Even on a picnic, it's essential to pack a cake, a sweet tart, or even ice cream to round off a wonderful meal. Ice cream may seem a little ambitious for a picnic, but, provided you have a good cooler with plenty of ice packs, it should be safe for a couple of hours before it succumbs to meltdown. I usually wrap the container in a layer of newspaper for extra insulation.

fresh figs with vin santo and mascarpone

1 cup mascarpone cheese

¼–½ cup confectioners' sugar, or to taste

⅓ cup Vin Santo, plus extra to serve

12 ripe figs

Serves 6

This lovely, simple dish is best served when you can find very good quality fresh figs, preferably straight from a tree. Vin Santo is an Italian sweet wine that marries well with the flavor of both the figs and the mascarpone—if you can't find it, you could also use port or cream sherry.

Put the mascarpone into a bowl, add the confectioners' sugar and Vin Santo, and beat until smooth. Set aside to infuse for 30 minutes, then transfer to a small serving bowl.

Cut the figs in half and arrange on a large serving platter with the bowl of mascarpone. Serve with the bottle of Vin Santo for people to help themselves.

meringues with rosewater cream

3 egg whites

⅓ cup sugar

¼ teaspoon ground cardamom

¾ cup heavy cream

1 tablespoon honey

1 tablespoon rosewater

pomegranate seeds, to serve (optional)

a baking sheet lined with wax paper

Serves 6

Rosewater is an exotic, fragrant aromatic widely used in Middle Eastern and North African cooking. It's sold in gourmet stores, some drugstores, and the baking sections of supermarkets. The meringues and rosewater cream are particularly good served with fresh pomegranate seeds, but work equally well with other fruits such as cherries, nectarines, or peaches.

Put the egg whites into a clean, dry bowl, and beat until they start to peak. Gradually beat in the sugar, a spoonful at a time, until the mixture becomes very thick and glossy. Fold in the ground cardamom.

Drop 12 spoonfuls of the meringue mixture onto the prepared baking sheet, leaving a gap between each mound. Bake in a preheated oven at 325°F for 1 hour. Remove from the oven, transfer the meringues to a wire rack, and let cool.

Put the cream, honey, and rosewater into a bowl and whip until the mixture just holds its shape. Put a couple of spoonfuls into each bowl, add the meringues, and top with the pomegranate seeds, if using.

caramelized **plum sorbet**

A refreshing and summery sorbet—pretty and delicious when served with thin, crisp, almond cookies. Roasting the plums before they are puréed will intensify their flavor.

2 lb. red plums, halved and pitted

2 tablespoons sugar

freshly squeezed juice of ½ lemon

sweet almond wafer cookies, to serve (optional)

Sugar syrup

1¼ cups sugar

1 vanilla bean, split lengthwise

Serves 6–8

Put the halved plums, cut side up, into an ovenproof dish, sprinkle with the sugar, and bake in a preheated oven at 400°F for 20 minutes until golden and softened. Let cool completely, then transfer to a blender, and purée until very smooth. Stir in the lemon juice.

Meanwhile, to make the sugar syrup, put the sugar and vanilla bean into a saucepan, add 2⅓ cups water, and heat gently until the sugar has dissolved. Bring to a boil, reduce the heat, and simmer for 5 minutes. Let cool, remove the vanilla bean, then stir the syrup into the plum purée.

Transfer to an ice cream maker and churn, according to the manufacturer's instructions. Store in the freezer until required.

Alternatively, transfer the purée to a plastic container and freeze for 5 hours, beating at hourly intervals with a balloon whisk. (This will break down the ice crystals and make the sorbet smooth.) Serve with the almond cookies, if using.

toasted coconut ice cream
with grilled pineapple

*Toasting the desiccated coconut enriches the ice cream and gives it
a lovely nutty flavor. Although in this recipe I serve it with wedges
of grilled pineapple, it works equally well with other fruits such
as mango or peaches.*

To make the ice cream, put the coconut into a dry skillet and toast, stirring over medium heat for 2–3 minutes until evenly browned. Transfer to a saucepan, then add the cream, coconut milk, and sugar. Heat gently until it just reaches boiling point.

Put the egg yolks into a bowl and beat with a wooden spoon until pale. Stir in about 2 tablespoons of the hot custard, then return the mixture to the pan. Heat gently, stirring constantly, until the mixture thickens enough to coat the back of the wooden spoon. Remove the pan from the heat and let cool completely.

When cold, strain the custard, and freeze in an ice cream maker according to the manufacturer's instructions. Transfer to the freezer until required.

Alternatively, pour the cold custard into a plastic container and freeze for 5 hours, beating at hourly intervals with a balloon whisk.

To prepare the pineapple, cut it lengthwise into wedges (including the leafy top) and remove the core sections. Put the sugar, butter, and rum into a small saucepan and heat until the sugar dissolves. Brush a little of the mixture over the pineapple wedges, then cook them on a preheated outdoor grill or on a stove-top grill pan for 2 minutes on each side until charred and tender. Remove from the heat and, holding the flesh with a fork, cut between the skin and flesh with a sharp knife. Cut the flesh into segments to make it easier to eat, then reassemble the wedges. Serve with the ice cream and remaining rum sauce, about 2 tablespoons each.

1 pineapple, medium or small, with leafy top if possible

½ cup brown sugar

1 stick unsalted butter

⅓ cup dark rum

Ice cream

⅓ cup dried unsweetened shredded coconut

1¾ cups heavy cream

1¼ cups coconut milk

½ cup sugar

5 egg yolks

Serves 6

pear gingerbread

4 ½ cups all-purpose flour

4 ¼ teaspoons baking powder

1 tablespoon ground ginger

½ teaspoon baking soda

½ teaspoon salt

¾ cup brown sugar

¾ cup unsalted butter

¾ cup molasses

¾ cup corn syrup

1 ¼ cups milk

1 egg, lightly beaten

2 large pears, peeled, cored, and diced

*a baking pan, 12 x 8 inches, greased
and bottom-lined with parchment*

Serves 12

Sift the flour, baking powder, ginger, baking soda, and salt into a large bowl. Put the sugar, butter, treacle, corn syrup, and milk into a saucepan and heat gently until the butter has melted and the sugar has dissolved.

Pour into the flour mixture, then add the egg, and beat with a wooden spoon until smooth. Fold in the diced pears, then spoon onto the prepared baking pan.

Transfer to a preheated oven and bake at 325°F for 1 ½ hours, or until a skewer inserted into the center comes out clean. Cool in the pan for 10 minutes, then let cool on a wire rack before serving.

The cooled cake may be wrapped in foil and stored in an airtight container for up to 5 days.

refrigerator
chocolate cake

14 oz. dark chocolate, chopped

½ cup unsalted butter

2 ½ cups Graham crackers, coarsely crushed

½ cup pine nuts

½ cup shelled pistachio nuts, coarsely chopped

½ cup candied ginger, coarsely chopped

1 cup unsweetened cocoa

1 teaspoon ground cinnamon

confectioners' sugar, to dust (optional)

*a springform cake pan, 9 x 3 inches diameter,
greased and bottom-lined with parchment*

Serves 12

Put the chocolate and butter into a bowl set over a saucepan of gently simmering water and heat gently until melted. Stir in all the remaining ingredients except the confectioners' sugar, then spoon into the prepared cake pan. Press the mixture well into the bottom and sides of the pan and smooth the surface with a spatula. Cover with foil and chill overnight.

When ready to serve, carefully work around the edges of the cake with a spatula and unmold onto a board, removing the paper from the bottom. Dust with confectioners' sugar, if using, and serve in thin fingers.

The cake may be stored in the refrigerator for up to 3 days.

lemon cake with vanilla syrup and strawberries

Vanilla syrup transforms this cake into a lovely dessert, but you can also serve it simply with a spoonful of yogurt.

1 stick unsalted butter, softened

1 cup sugar

2 lemons

2 eggs, lightly beaten

1¾ cups all-purpose flour

2 teaspoons baking powder

⅓ cup fine semolina

½ cup full-fat plain yogurt

fresh strawberries, to serve

Vanilla syrup

1 cup sugar

1 vanilla bean

a springform cake pan, 9 inches diameter, greased and bottom-lined with parchment

Serves 6

Grate the zest and squeeze the juice from the lemons. Put the butter, sugar, and lemon zest into a bowl and beat until pale and soft. Gradually beat in the eggs, a little at a time, until evenly mixed. Fold in the flour, baking powder, and semolina, then stir in the yogurt and lemon juice.

Spoon the mixture into the prepared cake pan and bake in a preheated oven at 350°F for about 40 minutes until risen and spongy. The cake is cooked when a toothpick inserted into the middle of the cake comes out clean. Cool in the pan

for about 5 minutes, then invert onto a wire rack to cool completely.

Meanwhile, to make the syrup, split the vanilla bean lengthwise with a sharp knife. Put the sugar and vanilla bean into a small saucepan and add 1¼ cups water. Heat gently until the sugar has dissolved. Bring to a boil and simmer for about 5 minutes, until it becomes syrupy. Remove from the heat and let cool a little.

To serve, cut the cake into slices while still slightly warm, pour over the syrup, and serve with strawberries.

drinks

No outdoor feast can be enjoyed without a tipple or two. Not that they have to be alcohol-based: cool smoothies and iced tea and coffee are all perfect. Remember, although smoothies are best immediately after blending, you can make them in advance and just give them a good shake up before drinking.

If you're having a large party, but don't want to serve just wine and don't have the manpower to prepare stick drinks and other cocktails en masse, try punch-style drinks such as Planter's Punch, summery Pimms, wine-based sangrias, or the endlessly popular Bloody Mary made in a big pitcher that can be constantly replenished.

What is a must, however, is the chill factor—serving lukewarm drinks on a hot day is no fun at all. If you're having a barbecue, organize big tubs of ice to take the drinks. If you're going on a picnic, pack the cooler with a bag of ice cubes, then put the drinks on top. If you're having a large party, hire extra freezers for ice and refrigerators for drinks, plus lots of glassware, allowing extra so you don't have to wash glasses in the middle of the party. Ask for the drinks to be delivered already cold, because it can take a long time to chill a large quantity of drinks or to freeze ice yourself. Then chill out, al fresco!

iced ginger tea

When making iced tea, it's best to add the tea bags to cold water rather than boiling water in order to avoid the unpleasant scum that can appear on the surface. So boil the water, then let it cool before adding the tea.

2-inch piece of fresh ginger, peeled
and finely sliced
4 tea bags (I prefer Indian tea)
2 limes, sliced
ice cubes
lemon soda or lemonade

Serves 6

Put the sliced ginger into a large pitcher, pour over 1 quart boiling water, and let cool. Add the tea bags and chill for 1 hour.

Strain the tea into a clean pitcher, add the slices of lime and ice, then top up with lemon soda or lemonade.

iced lemon coffee

Iced lemon coffee can be just as refreshing as as iced lemon tea on a hot day. It may sound a little strange, but it's very thirst-quenching.

2 cups freshly brewed espresso coffee
sugar, to taste
ice cubes
1 tablespoon freshly squeezed
lemon juice
lemon peel, to serve

Serves 6

Pour the coffee into a large pitcher, add sugar to taste, and stir until dissolved. Let cool, then chill until very cold.

Half-fill glasses with ice cubes. Add the lemon juice to the coffee, then pour into the glasses, and serve with a twist of lemon peel.

strawberry and banana
ice cream shake

A great shake for those times when you're in serious ice cream mode. Other fruits also marry well with the banana—try mango and banana with vanilla ice cream, or raspberry and banana with raspberry ice cream.

2 cups ripe strawberries, hulled

1 ripe banana, peeled and chopped

4 scoops strawberry ice cream, plus extra to serve (optional)

¾ cup milk

Serves 3–4

Put the strawberries, banana, ice cream, and milk into a blender and purée until very smooth. Pour into glasses and serve topped with extra ice cream, if using.

lemon soda with mint and bitters

A delightfully simple drink, ideal for hot summer days. The Bitters give the lemon soda a refreshing, herbal flavor and make it a pretty pale pink.

1 quart lemon soda or lemonade

6 sprigs of mint

Angostura Bitters

lemon slices

ice cubes

Serves 6

Pour the lemon soda or lemonade into 6 tall glasses, adding a sprig of mint to each one.

Add a few drops of Bitters, a few slices of lemon and ice cubes, then serve at once.

stick drinks

Stick drinks, also known as caprioskas, are cocktails made by mashing fruits and sugar together with a stick, usually a frozen treat stick, or, as I prefer, a citrus press. You can use almost any fruit as long as you include chopped limes and sugar. These are two of my favorites.

lime and mint stick drink

12 large mint leaves
2 teaspoons brown sugar
1 lime, finely diced, including skin
ice cubes
2 large shots Bacardi rum
club soda

cocktail shaker or pitcher
2 cocktail glasses

Serves 2

Put the mint leaves, sugar, and lime into a shaker or pitcher and mash with a stick or spoon until quite pulpy. Alternatively, use a mortar and pestle.

Fill 2 glasses with ice to chill them thoroughly, then tip the ice into the mashed mint mixture. Add the Bacardi to the mixture, shake well, then pour back into the glasses. Add a little club soda and serve.

kiwifruit, passionfruit, and lime stick drink

1 large lime, diced
1 large kiwifruit, peeled and diced
12 mint leaves
3 teaspoons sugar
1 large passionfruit, halved
ice cubes
2 large shots vodka

cocktail shaker or pitcher
2 cocktail glasses

Serves 2

Put the lime and kiwifruit into a shaker or pitcher, add the mint, sugar, and passionfruit pulp and seeds. Mash well until pulpy.

Fill 2 glasses with ice to chill them thoroughly, then tip the ice into the kiwifruit mixture. Add the vodka, shake or stir well, then pour back into the glasses.

outdoor parties

A cocktail party can be an exercise in logistics. If your party is outdoors, here are a few things to keep in mind:

Food
• Serve 4–6 canapes per person, per hour.
• Keep food hot or cold: danger zone is 40–150°F. The most dangerous is about 85°F, the temperature of a hot kitchen!
• If people are juggling a drink, a plate, and a napkin, make it easy—serve foods they can eat with their fingers or a fork.

Drinks
• Better too much than too little—some suppliers will let you return what you don't use—and don't forget the non-drinkers.
Champagne For a 2-hour party, allow ½ bottle each, ¾ bottle for 3 hours (6 glasses in a bottle, or 8 if making cocktails).
Wine ¾–1 bottle per person (serve the leftovers at your next dinner party). In summer, allow 3 bottles of white to 1 of red.
Liquor and cocktails 16 measures in a 1-fifth bottle of liquor. Allow 3 per person during a 2-hour party.
Punches Strong ones, such as Planter's Punch, contain about the same amount of alcohol as a measure of liquor, so cater as for liquor. Wine-based punches, such as sangria, are only a little weaker than wine, so cater as for wine.
Mineral water and soft drinks Don't forget the non-drinkers, "designated drivers," and kids. Have lots and keep it cold.

PARTY COUNTDOWN
One week ahead
• Order drinks, glasses, ice, ice buckets, and containers for ice, drinks, and garbage.
• Arrange shade, music, candles, and insect repellent.
• Organize kitchen equipment for your chosen menu—hire extra freezers and refrigerators if necessary.
• Prepare dishes to be frozen until the day.

Two or three days ahead
• Prepare ice creams, wrap cakes, buy ready-to-roll dough.
• Check with suppliers and caterers.

One day ahead
• Buy all the food, except the most perishable.
• Prepare meats, sauces, and marinades and chill overnight.
• Assemble skewers of seafood, chicken, or meat, keeping bamboo wet until ready to cook.
• Cook dishes such as cold meats to be chilled overnight.
• Prepare basic mixtures for drinks such as punch.
• Arrange seating and tables, check linen and napkins, and collect bar equipment indoors (corkscrews, glasses, etc.)
• Put the drinks in the refrigerator to chill.

Morning of party
• Buy foods such as salad leaves, herbs, creams, etc.
• Prepare dressings and salsas.
• Prepare vegetables and cover with plastic wrap.
• Assemble dishes that are able to stand, then cover and chill.

One hour ahead
• Assemble and cook all dishes except those needing last-minute cooking.
• If any of the food is going to be grilled, light the coals—they should have reached the right temperature in about 40–45 minutes.

Thirty minutes ahead
• Preheat the oven, uncork wines, prepare materials for cocktails.

When the first guest arrives
• Pull the champagne corks and start serving the cocktails.

the best barbecue

Outdoor grills come in all shapes, sizes, varieties, and prices, from small disposable aluminum ones sold in supermarkets, to large, high-tech covered gas or electric grills. Some grills have both a grill and a flat plate offering versatility, but this is not essential. A windshield is a great advantage.

Cooking on a charcoal grill
• Charcoal grills use either standard briquettes or hardwood lump charcoal. The former may contain chemicals from the process used to make them, which, though totally safe, may affect the flavor of the food. I prefer hardwood lump charcoal, which, though not as readily available, contains no additives, burns easily, gets far hotter, and lasts longer.
• Arrange the fuel at least 4 inches deep in as large an area as possible, leaving a little room around the edges.
• Put a few barbecue lighters in between the coals and light them with a taper or matches.
• Let the coals burn for 40–45 minutes until the flames have subsided and the coals are covered in gray ash. To test the heat, hold your hand 5 inches above the fire and count how long it can stay there. A hot fire will be a couple seconds, a medium-hot fire 3–4 seconds, and a cool fire 5–6 seconds.
• Many grills have adjustable rungs—the closest to the heat is the hottest, and the furthest away obviously the coolest.

Cooking on gas or electric grills
• For proper browning, preheat until very hot before adding the food, then reduce the heat as necessary.
• They can be adjusted in the same way as a domestic stove, by turning the temperature up or down.
• They are often available with a hood, to cover the food as it grills (a similar effect to roasting).

Portable grills
• A wide selection of styles is available, fueled by either charcoal or gas. Remember, coals stay hot for some time, so dispose of them legally and safely, or wait until they are totally cold before carefully packing them in a bag to take with you.
• Set the grill up on level ground and never move it once lit.
• Safety is extremely important: in some places, grills will constitute a fire risk. Be sensible and set it up away from dry timber or grass and always take a fire blanket or a small portable fire extinguisher with you.

Cleaning
• Clean the grill as soon as possible after cooking, while it is still assembled and any residual bits of food stuck there can be brushed off into the fire.
• Do not clean the grill with soap or water, just scrub well with a wire brush (see equipment below). After cleaning, rub the flat plate with a little oil to season it and stop rust.
• If you have a gas or electric grill, clean in the same way. Special cleaners are also available.

Basic grilling equipment
• Long-handled tongs, so you don't burn yourself (don't leave them on or near the heat as they can get very hot).
• Bamboo or metal skewers. Metal can get very hot, so turn using a dishcloth or tongs. Bamboo skewers are disposable and must be presoaked before use, to stop them burning.
• A sturdy wire brush for cleaning.

Food safety
• Grilled food takes longer to cook: cook pork and poultry thoroughly and don't start cooking until the coals are ready.

the perfect picnic

Choose a spot that's easy to get to, preferably close to where you can park your car. It's all very well planning a romantic picnic at the top of a mountain, but don't forget that a picnic basket can get very heavy, very quickly!

Comfort
• If you have a big car, take light, collapsible tables and chairs.
• Take plenty of blankets and pillows.
• Choose a shady place to spread your picnic blanket.
• Take lanterns, flashlights, and citronella tea-lights for evening.

Storage
• Safety and convenience are the most important elements.
• Use coolers. Pack the base with freezer blocks and put raw ingredients on the bottom and more delicate ones on top. This is also the best method for carrying ice cubes.
• Refrigerate precooked or prepared food until ready to pack.
• Remove marinated meat or fish from the refrigerator 1 hour before cooking and return to room temperature. It will cook more quickly, reducing the risk of undercooking and spoiling.
• Chill and store the food in the same container; plastic containers, zip-lock bags, and vacuum flasks are all good. Plastic or glass bottles are good for drinks, dressings, or syrups.
• Wrap sandwiches and rolls in wax paper, then in foil. Store and transport cakes in their pans.
• Hardware and office supply stores sell aluminum storage pans. Cookware stores and Asian stores also sell stackable stainless steel lunch boxes—ideal for small snack dishes.

Transport
• Picnic baskets are romantic, but often impractical. When full, they're very heavy and hard for one person to carry. I prefer a two-handled basket to share the load.
• Use paper plates and plastic cups—or glasses and plates wrapped individually in paper towels or cloth to avoid breakage.
• For adventurous picnics, pack non-perishable foods that can be eaten with your fingers. For easy transport, use a backpack.

index

conversion charts

Weights and measures have been rounded up or down slightly to make measuring easier.

volume equivalents

american	metric	imperial
1 teaspoon	5 ml	
1 tablespoon	15 ml	
¼ cup	60 ml	2 fl.oz.
⅓ cup	75 ml	2½ fl.oz.
½ cup	125 ml	4 fl.oz.
⅔ cup	150 ml	5 fl.oz. (¼ pint)
¾ cup	175 ml	6 fl.oz.
1 cup	250 ml	8 fl.oz.

weight equivalents:

imperial	metric
1 oz.	25 g
2 oz.	50 g
3 oz.	75 g
4 oz.	125 g
5 oz.	150 g
6 oz.	175 g
7 oz.	200 g
8 oz. (½ lb)	250 g
9 oz.	275 g
10 oz.	300 g
11 oz.	325 g
12 oz.	375 g
13 oz.	400 g
14 oz.	425 g
15 oz.	475 g
16 oz. (1 lb.)	500 g
2 1b.	1 kg

measurements:

inches	cm
¼ inch	5 mm
½ inch	1 cm
¾ inch	1.5 cm
1 inch	2.5 cm
2 inches	5 cm
3 inches	7 cm
4 inches	10 cm
5 inches	12 cm
6 inches	15 cm
7 inches	18 cm
8 inches	20 cm
9 inches	23 cm
10 inches	25 cm
11 inches	28 cm
12 inches	30 cm

oven temperatures:

225°F	110°C	Gas ¼
250°F	120°C	Gas ½
275°F	140°C	Gas 1
300°F	150°C	Gas 2
325°F	160°C	Gas 3
350°F	180°C	Gas 4
375°F	190°C	Gas 5
400°F	200°C	Gas 6
425°F	220°C	Gas 7
450°F	230°C	Gas 8
475°F	240°C	Gas 9